MOVING FORWARD
STAYING CATHOLIC IN COLLEGE

Cover design & Photography by Laura Womack.

Copy editing by Natalie Alemán and Danielle Rzepka.

Special thanks to all those who have contributed to this piece in its original form.

ISBN: 978-0-9853575-2-8

Published by Life Teen, Inc.
2222 S. Dobson Rd.
Suite 601
Mesa, AZ 85202
www.lifeteen.com

Printed in the United States of America.
Printed on acid-free paper.

For more information about Life Teen or to order additional copies, go online to www.lifeteen.com or call us at 1-800-809-3902.

DEDICATION

This book is dedicated to all those young souls who have bravely moved forward into college unashamed to live out their Catholic faith.

Remember that whenever you boldly live out your faith to the sounds of mockery on earth, there is applause in heaven.

TABLE OF
CONTENTS

INTRODUCTION

BY MATT SMITH

Finally, college is here.

If you're anything like me, you've been looking forward to this for a long time. I knew I was meant for college in the fifth grade. Everyone else in my class was into kid video games, kid TV shows, kid stuff. Not me. My favorite TV shows were sitcoms about college. So what if I hadn't even taken pre-algebra yet? I knew I was destined for the university life.

I don't know what exactly attracted me to college. Maybe it was the fact that I was in a small rural town, and college campuses were a part of a vibrant city life. Or maybe I was attracted to the interwoven relationships and the exciting college TV drama. They were by far much more engaging than the dull school days with my 10-year-old friends. As I recall, the only thing exciting that happened that year was when the girl that I was crushing on asked me if she could wear my jacket. (For the record, she gave it back to me at the end of the day. Love hurts.)

My best guess, though, is that what drew me to college was the idea of being grown up and independent. College would be that exciting time in my life where I could hug my parents goodbye, hop in the car, and drive off into the sunset, destined for a new life on campus. I thought about this sending off through each year of high school.

COLLEGE TURNED OUT TO BE A LOT HARDER THAN I HAD EXPECTED.

Sure enough, my time came and went pretty much just like that. Everything after that, however, was completely unscripted. College turned out to be a lot harder than I had expected. Unlike those old TV shows, I knew that college would have tough professors and demanding schedules – but I never expected the punishing workload that would be given on Day One. I never expected to study day after day just to get a B in a course. College was filled with surprises.

However, what was most surprising to me was how many of my Christian friends from high school would lose their faith in college. We seemed so like one another when we went *into* college; but four years later, we could not have been more different.

Looking back at college from the comfort of adulthood, the only way I can make sense of what happened is through Scripture:

> *"A sower went out to sow. And as he sowed, some seed fell on the path, and birds came and ate it up. Some fell on rocky ground, where it had little soil. It sprang up at once because the soil was not deep, and when the sun rose it was scorched, and it withered for lack of roots. Some seed fell among thorns, and the thorns grew up and choked it. But some seed fell on rich soil, and produced fruit, a hundred or sixty or thirtyfold. Whoever has ears ought to hear."*
>
> - Matthew 13: 3-9

This common verse (you've probably heard it dozens of times) explains very clearly how the seed – which is the Gospel itself – takes root in our hearts. It basically predicts what will happen to your faith in life, but especially in college. Let's talk through your four options. (I've underlined some words for emphasis.)

OPTION 1: THE DOUBTER

> *"The seed sown on the path is the one who hears the word of the kingdom without <u>understanding</u> it, and the evil one comes and steals away what was sown in his heart."*
>
> - Matthew 13:19

You went to church with your family, but all along you had your doubts. On your worst days, you thought the whole "God thing" was a fairytale – it made a good story, but it doesn't make a lot of sense in the real world. Scripture verses contradict themselves, crazy things happen in the Bible, and Church teaching seems to be all about rules and not about God.

These are all common misunderstandings that some people carry with them into college. Many Christians get tripped up because their faith that took shape in high school seems too simple and insufficient when compared the big new world of college.

Doubts shouldn't threaten your faith; they should motivate you with curiosity to go deeper. Because the answers are there – waiting – but only for those who seek to understand.

DOUBTS SHOULDN'T THREATEN YOUR FAITH.

Let's move on to your second option.

OPTION 2: THE GRABBER

"The seed sown among thorns is the one who hears the word, but then <u>worldly anxiety and the lure of riches</u> choke the word and it bears no fruit."

– Matthew 13:22

I believe there are two very different halves of the college experience. Your freshman and sophomore years are about getting *comfortable* with the life of a college student:

- Did I get into the classes that I want?
- Am I prepared for class today?
- Did I do well on my midterm? My final?

Then in the second half, during your junior and senior years, you get more *uncomfortable* about your life after college. Worldly anxiety creeps in about who you are and how you compare to others:

- What is my GPA? Is it good enough?
- Will my degree get me the job I want at the salary I need?
- What kind of grades do I need to get an internship with a top company?
- How can I beat out my peers for that top job after graduation?

It's troubling that something that starts so pure – trying to be a good student – can quickly become an obsession. Success becomes your new god. Don't let a fascination for success, glory, and prestige overtake your fascination with the Everlasting God.

OPTION 3: THE PUSHOVER

"The seed sown on rocky ground is the one who hears the word and receives it at once with joy. But he has no root and lasts only for a time. When some <u>tribulation or persecution</u> comes because of the world, he immediately falls away."

- Matthew 13: 20-21

This part of the parable is pretty easy to understand: if your roots don't grow deep, you have no chance of surviving. College will be a test of how deep your Catholic roots go.

When you experience <u>tribulation</u>, your life gets flipped upside down because of great trouble or suffering. Because you are now independent and away from the support of your parents, trials in college can feel larger than life itself. For example: during my freshman year of college, my very expensive sound system was stolen from my car in a parking deck right next to my dorm. In the moment, that was a very difficult thing to deal with. I felt vulnerable and humiliated. What was next? What else could get stolen?

Then there were the breakups during my sophomore and senior years – two big, messy, heart-wrenching breakups. In the classroom, I was challenged by difficult courses that drove me to study through sleepless nights.

Through all of these tribulations, I found comfort in God, yet so many of my Christian friends looked for consolation elsewhere: the social life, partying, dating, whatever. And just like Scripture warned, "they immediately [fell] away" (Matthew 13:21).

> **SO MANY OF MY CHRISTIAN FRIENDS LOOKED FOR CONSOLATION ELSEWHERE.**

Tribulation may challenge many young Catholics, but for most of us, we know that trial is coming. Nobody said that college would be easy. What's surprising to most Catholics coming into college is the amount of persecution that comes your way. Let me tell you want to expect. You will be persecuted by two groups of people in two different ways:

From Professors:

We're in a strange time in society here at the beginning of the Third Millennium. There is a quiet but deep-rooted hostility towards Catholicism on most college campuses. By that, I mean that there is a climate created from curricula, coursework, and professors that allows for open discrimination against Christians. Any tenant of Christian morality is subject to harsh criticism, especially in liberal arts courses: psychology, sociology, history, literature, etc. (I've never known of a calculus professor to mock Christianity.) If this trend continues to gain momentum, Christianity will soon be the *only* religion that can be openly disrespected, mocked, and ridiculed by peers and professors all within the safety of the classroom.

Persecution is very difficult to deal with as a student, because professors obviously have more education than you do. They can be persuasive and make you feel duped because of your choice to follow any part of Christianity. Plus it's hard to argue with a professor when you know that it could hurt your grade or make your life difficult. In the end, just know that professors who bully students by disrespecting their beliefs are abusing their power. Pray for them and don't lose faith.

From Peers:

There is a huge subculture in college that is all about partying. It goes something like this: *alcohol, loud music, marijuana, hooking up. Repeat.* The difference between partying in high school and in college is that now everyone's parents are gone. This allows for partying to be central to the social life. Many fraternities and sororities have built their identities around the party lifestyle. You'll see this on display in your first weeks on campus as "rush" begins. It can get intense and it will feel like everyone is out partying.

Even if you don't go the Greek route, alcohol, drugs, and sex can become

> **I SPENT A LOT OF TIME ALONE MY FIRST SEMESTER IN COLLEGE, BUT IT WAS WORTH IT.**

central to groups of peers. I cannot overstate this. One Friday during my freshman year of college, I couldn't find a single friend to hang out with because everyone was planning on getting drunk. That wasn't easy. I spent a lot of time alone my first semester in college, but it was worth it.

When you stand up against your professors or stand out from your peers, you should expect to be persecuted. It is going to happen and it won't be easy. Persecution is never easy: you are stressed, you feel like your group of friends is divided against you, you doubt yourself because life was easier before you stood up for yourself, and you're confused about what will happen next.

Of course you can avoid all of this if you're a *Pushover*. You just go with the flow. You'll stand for nothing and you'll fall for anything.

OPTION 4: THE STRONG ONE

"But the seed sown on rich soil is the one who hears the word and understands it, who indeed <u>bears fruit</u> and yields a hundred or sixty or thirtyfold."

–Matthew 13:23

YOU DON'T HAVE TO FIT IN BECAUSE YOU ARE A CHILD OF GOD.

Your final option in college is to let your Catholic faith grow and flourish. Unlike the *Doubter* (option 1), you explore your Catholic faith to find answers to your questions. You excel through each semester, but unlike the *Grabber* (option 2), you keep your priorities straight by first focusing on God. You are stronger than the *Pushover* (option 3) because you rely on God when you experience tribulation and persecution; you refuse to be dominated by popular opinion.

While in college, you won't waste your time trying to fit in. (When does that ever work?) You don't have to fit in because you are a child of God. Sometimes that means you'll be liked, other times you'll be disliked, and you'll often be misunderstood. These things happen regardless of *what* you stand for, so why not stand up for the Truth?

The best part is this: while peers are fumbling through their years of college trying to find out who they are and what they stand for, your audacity to stand out will give them hope. It will make them wonder about what gives you such grace and confidence. This is why Scripture tells us that our rich faith will yield so much fruit.

SUMMARY

In college you will find people who oppose your beliefs and who want to discourage you in your faith walk. But, Pope Benedict puts it well, "Dear young people, you are a precious gift for society. Do not yield to discouragement in the face of difficulties." You are capable of being the *Strong One* (option 4), and we encourage you to be open to the ways that God will speak to you through this book.

Although every person's college experience will look different, you'll find as you read this book that there are practical pieces of wisdom that you can draw from in each part.

In this book you'll find practical advice from Catholics who've gone before you and who sincerely want you to have a great experience in college. Even if you're the only person living out your Catholic faith, or if you're one of many, we firmly believe that you have the capability of being a witness on your campus. You are not the future of the Church; you are the Church at this present moment. Don't be afraid to stand out and be a mature disciple of Christ wherever He has called you to go after high school.

CHAPTER ONE:
NEWFOUND FREEDOM

BY MARK HART

I remember the blindingly bright light seeping through the plane's windows. I remember the nervousness I felt as the cabin door closed. I remember the heartbreak I felt kissing my girlfriend goodbye. I remember the weight of responsibility I felt to make my priest, youth minister, and Core Members proud. I remember how overwhelmed I was at the proposition of moving 2,000 miles away from home at just 17 years old and not knowing a soul on my new campus home.

It was on that flight that it all set in for the very first time.

No one knew me. What I'd accomplished in high school didn't matter anymore… *everyone* at my new university had accomplished things. The image and reputation I'd spent four years of high school crafting was now meaningless. My test scores were inconsequential; my Varsity letters worth less than the free peanuts the flight attendant was peddling. I would soon be surrounded by souls who didn't know the high school version of myself, who had no idea of the moral lows and spiritual highs I'd experienced to date. "I can reinvent myself," I thought. No one there would be able to judge me for my teenage failures, true; but sadly, no one would be able to celebrate my spiritual transformation with me, either.

When I was reintroduced to Christ my junior year of high school, I was forced to make a decision. Would I continue on my path of self-centeredness, or would I take the path far less traveled and follow Christ? After wrestling with the Lord, I chose to walk with God and I didn't look back (Luke 9:62).

Here I was now, embarking on a new journey of faith. The plane touched down. The cab dropped me off on campus. I stood at the

WHICH PATH ARE YOU GOING TO TAKE?

front of the sprawling quads before me and watched the sidewalks drift into every conceivable direction. There was a new path being put before me, diverging into the future. It was another opportunity – another decision – I was being asked to make: would I seek my own desires in college or seek God?

That first step forward on the path, and every step that followed, was a decision that would ultimately lead me closer to or further from God.

Which path are you going to take?

DECISIONS, DECISIONS

The following story depicts well the modern collegiate struggle, I think:

Deep in the country lived a very wise man. The man's son appreciated his father's wisdom, but as the years wore on and the son grew older, he also grew tired of his father always having the right answer.

One day the son devised a plan to confuse and defeat his father in a match of wits. The boy captured a bird and hid it in his hands. Knowing the father would correctly ascertain that the object in his hands was a bird, the son would then ask his father if the bird was dead or alive.

If he said the bird was alive, the son would crush the bird in his hands, so that when he opened his hands the bird would be dead. But, if the father said the bird was dead, the son would open his hands and let the bird fly free.

That evening, as the father came in from the fields, the son ran out to meet him asking, "Father, what is it that I have in my hands?"

The father said, "You have a bird, my son."

The son then asked, "Father, tell me: Is the bird alive or is it dead?"

The father looked at the son, thought for a moment and said, "The answer is in your hands."

Life brings with it a series of decisions. Every day, in fact, every second you are living out a decision you made. College is no different.

Do I get up or hit snooze again?
Do I shower or not?
Do I get ready or just opt for the sweats and a cap?
Do I go to that class or grab a coffee instead?
Do I use my meal plan or just opt for Ramen, again?
Do I go over to their room or just hang out in my own?
Do I start on that paper or defend my title on the Xbox?
Do I confront my roommate or just keep the peace?
Do I stay in tonight or head out?
Do I order that pizza at midnight or just go to bed?
Do I head to Mass on Sunday, or am I "just too tired"?

Some of these decisions appear minimal and seemingly carry no consequence beyond the moment. Others will affect you throughout the semester and even in the years to come.

Some decisions speak to long-term goals, others to personal wounds, and still others to your desire (or lack thereof) for holiness. Some decisions bring life; many bring death. I'm not saying this metaphorically, either. Scripture attests to this truth (see Deuteronomy 30:15-19).

You see, your body and your soul (or "your flesh and your spirit" as St. Paul puts it in Romans chapters 7 and 8) can easily become embroiled in a tug of war that places both your current joy and your lasting salvation on the line.

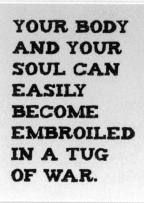

YOUR BODY AND YOUR SOUL CAN EASILY BECOME EMBROILED IN A TUG OF WAR.

In the midst of this tug-of-war breathes the Holy Spirit, constantly speaking to your heart, pointing you toward the light of Christ, and inviting you to true and lasting freedom.

TRUE FREEDOM

Many souls in this world shortsightedly believe that the highest form of **freedom** is "doing whatever you want, whenever you want." They're typically the ones whose hair you'll end up holding as they celebrate that "freedom," on all fours, worshiping the porcelain god after a night of binge drinking and utter inebriation.

Those who believe college "frees" them from the constraints of their adolescent lives are usually the same ones totally devastated by broken relationships in which they sacrificed their body, soul, and dignity on an altar of lust, "acceptance," and false love, only to be used and discarded by another.

Those who think "freedom" allows them no accountability are the ones who often find themselves failing classes, immersed in debt, morally bankrupt, or looking to the future with little hope and no leads after squandering years of time and money on campus in search for their next party.

Think about it. How do you define freedom?

> ## IF YOU CAN'T SAY NO TO SOMETHING, THAN YOUR "YES" MEANS ABSOLUTELY NOTHING.

If you can't say no to something, are you really free? If you can't say no to sex, or to getting drunk, or to drugs, how is that freedom? Put simply, it's not. If you can't, or won't, say "no" to something, you are enslaved by it or by the desire for it. If you can't say no to something, than your "yes" means absolutely nothing.

Blessed John Paul II put it this way, "Freedom consists not in doing what we like, but in having the right to do what we ought." And St. Augustine – who could have taught a Master's Level course about sin – took this truth even further, reminding Christians, "In doing what we ought we deserve no praise, because it is our duty."

As a son or daughter of God, you most boldly proclaim and exercise your freedom by living a life of virtue and humility that not only brings you true peace but also deep joy. Now, this doesn't mean that every moment will bring happiness. To be sure, living the Christian life is difficult – it requires your whole life. Saying you are a Catholic will cost you very little, but living like a true Catholic in today's culture will cost you everything. If you want to live for heaven, you must be willing to die to many earthly things.

You must be on the lookout, too; "your adversary the devil prowls around like a roaring **lion**, seeking some one to devour" (1 Peter 5:8). Put simply, if you're seeking God, the enemy is seeking you (Romans 7:21). His strategy is to exploit your weaknesses, and sin enters most frequently through the doors we intentionally leave open.

SIN CAN BE SUBTLE

Sin is death. Jesus said it (Luke 12:5). St. Paul echoed it (Romans 6:23). The Church warns us about it (CCC 1035, 1488). The saints believed it and lived like it. One thing that the saints all had in common is that they feared sin (spiritual death) more than physical death.

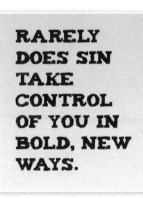

RARELY DOES SIN TAKE CONTROL OF YOU IN BOLD, NEW WAYS.

Rarely does sin take control of you in bold, new ways. Sin is welcomed in through smaller entry points that grow deeper over time. What begins with missing Sunday Mass can, over time, turn into an abandonment of one's faith (and values). What starts with a little chemical experimentation often evolves into a full-blown addiction. "That one night" of blowing off homework, that one day of missed classes, or that occasional "drunken hookup" quickly become more habit than exception.

Sins become friends and are invited to move into the dorm room. Once there, they set up shop in your life and lay roots in your soul. The snowball of shame and guilt will grow heavier until your moral compass is pointing only toward self. All of a sudden, the beauty and peace you knew during your high school youth group days are labeled as "just a phase" as you seek to protect sinful desires and justify destructive habits. "So what if I'm underage," or "It's just weed," or "It's only oral sex" are all phrases that began with smaller, seemingly insignificant moral compromises. The road to hell is paved with small acts of selfishness and pride.

St. John Chrysostom compared our five senses (taste, touch, smell, hearing, and sight) to the entry points of a majestic castle. You must guard those entry points steadily, protecting your castle at all costs from the enemy. The devil will use every medium and take any opportunity to violate our pursuit of sanctity; he uses the totality of creation to turn us away from the Creator. Those things we can taste and touch, see, hear, and smell can either pull us toward darkness or inspire us to run toward the light.

Think about it. Pornography is an entry point. Chemical abuse is an entry point. Sloth and laziness are entry points. Immodesty is an entry point. The list is endless.

Likewise, there are tons of opportunities to grow in grace. How many of those do you frequently see lived out in a college setting? How many will you seek out? How far are you willing to go socially to insure that you maintain your integrity personally?

This isn't to say that every situation you find yourself in will lead you to hell – not at all. However, like the young son holding the bird, the choice is in your hands. The decisions you make socially in college are absolutely life or death choices. Each day you have the chance to choose life (God's way) or death (the world's way). The consequences of decisions made in your first semester will often still be ringing well into your last semester.

So how do you ensure that – as you're standing before our heavenly Father – you're choosing life within the situations He places in your hands?

CHAPTER TWO:
DECISIONS, DECISIONS

BY JACKIE FRANÇOIS

Every new chapter in life brings with it new opportunities to make decisions to become the man or woman God is calling you to be. Whether or not you liked who you were in high school, there's always room to grow in virtue and to become an even better version of yourself, the one God always designed you to become (Ephesians 2:10). College is not a chance to put on a new "face," but it is an opportunity to form new friendships and community, learn new concepts, and to accept new challenges that will help you grow. Granted, "new" is not always better, but these new experiences will stretch your heart, mind, and soul to a capacity you never thought possible, regardless of the struggle that may come with it.

When it comes to dealing with challenges, many college students choose the "easy" way out by partying, drinking, hooking-up, and slacking-off. Unfortunately for those students, what could have been a worthwhile college experience becomes a waste of (a lot of) time and money. Every challenge that comes your way should lead you to ask yourself, "How can this help me grow in holiness?" Surely, every challenge provides the opportunity to grow in virtue, whether it is a stodgy professor, an annoying roommate, or a demanding course. When you see the opportunity for growth in these trials, you will indeed grow in virtue. Every decision you make, as a result, will either lead you closer to heaven or hell (no pressure).

Seriously, though, our decisions do matter. We can either let the culture sway and form us or let Christ's grace aid and transform us. The former will enslave us to sin, but the latter will free us to love and live life abundantly, with great joy and peace (John 10:10). One way to know you're making the "right" decision (although there may be a few ways to make the "right" decision) in a given situation is if you have peace and joy. Now, obviously, some situations carry more weight than others. You might not feel grave anxiety within your heart if you decide to choose Captain Crunch over Wheaties for breakfast (although you might feel a grave pain in your stomach). However, if you choose to get drunk with a group of friends at a party rather than have a light-hearted movie night with a different group of friends, you might notice a lack of peace and joy in your heart. Or if you choose to be in a relationship with someone who is leading you to sin, you might notice that you justify that relationship with a lot of "but's," while knowing deep in your heart that something "just isn't right."

AN ABSENCE OF PEACE MIGHT BE GOD'S WAY OF GETTING YOU TO PRAY MORE.

Peace and joy are fruits of the Holy Spirit and they allow us to know we are following God's will. An absence of peace might be God's way of getting you to pray more or, even more likely, could be an indicator that you are not in rhythm with His will. On the other hand, anxiety is a human feeling that lets us know we are not in the right place/state of being/relationship. When we feel anxiety, God tells us to listen to it. The devil, however, tells us to ignore it. More than anything, God wants the best for us (see Jeremiah 29:11-13), and He wants us to know that His love is better than anything we could ever experience in this life (Psalm 63:2-3).

DESOLATION TURNS US IN ON OURSELVES TO FOCUS ON THE NEGATIVE THINGS IN OUR LIFE.

When we make decisions, we can ask ourselves, "Is this decision leading me closer to God or away from him?" This is a major theme of Ignatian discernment; some decisions lead us to consolation, and thus lead us to God and allow us to be a gift to love others selflessly. Decisions that lead us to desolation turn us away from God and from the community that will lead us closer to Him. Desolation turns us in on ourselves to focus on the negative things in our life, clouding a hopeful perspective that we are made for more than this moment;

desolation sometimes causes spiritual amnesia, where we forget that we are made for heaven and focus only on the pleasures of the "now." It is only through prayer and a relationship with the Holy Spirit that this peace and joy will dwell deeply within you. As you go through college, let the Holy Spirit be your guide, and everything will be alright.

DEALING WITH HOMESICKNESS

I'm sure you've heard the saying, "Home is where the heart is." Well, this saying may be quite helpful in making your new school a cozy home for your heart to dwell. Although it's always difficult to be far from family and friends, my hope is that your roommates won't find you curled up in a ball, shaking, foaming at the mouth, clicking your heels, and longing for "home."

Here are some tips to avoid (or deal with) homesickness:

- Find a good young community at school or in a local church.
- Keep in touch with family and friends via Skype, email, and regular mail (who doesn't like getting an actual letter, right?)
- Schedule when you are going to visit home and stick to it.
- Encourage family or friends to visit once a semester, if possible.
- Pray: Daily Mass, Adoration, or meditate with the Rosary.
- If you have a lot of anxiety or fear, visit the school counselor or psychologist (most of the time, counseling is offered for free) to help you out.

FINDING, LIVING, AND COPING WITH ROOMMATES

Living with others is *always* a challenge, whether it's your family, spouse, or new college roommates. Different personalities, expectations, boundaries, and lifestyles usually make living with others a constant challenge and call to patience and humility, if not also laughter and hilarity. Whether your college lets you list preferences for roommates or just throws a bunch of random people together, some find their best friends from being college roommates, and some find their least favorite person in the world (who they hope to never smell again). The idea of sharing rooms and/or bathrooms may be completely foreign to you if you come from a small family or if you're an only child. On the other hand, if you come from a big family, you may have more space and privacy than ever before! Either way, here are some helpful tips to help you find, live, and cope with your roommates:

Finding a Roommate:
If you are allowed to list qualities or attributes you would like to have in a roommate, be specific. Maybe you want your roommate to be in the same major as you so you can study together. Hopefully you want your roommates to share your faith, and you list "Catholic" or "Christian" as an important requirement. Maybe you're vegan or celiac or the scent of a peanut makes your face explode and you want to live with someone who shares your dietary needs. The more specific you are in the beginning, the less hassle you'll have when trying to explain to your R.A. why you can't live with a pagan-worshiping, peanut-loving, trumpet major.

Living with a Roommate:
If you are having very serious issues with your roommate(s), do not hesitate to ask to be moved. If your roommates are getting drunk all the time, doing drugs, or bringing their boyfriend or girlfriend to spend the night, say something to your R.A. If they're doing something illegal (like drinking or doing drugs), report it, even if you feel a lot of pressure to not be a "narc." These people should be leading you closer to heaven and not closer to handcuffs and a jail cell. If your roommate is sleeping with their boyfriend or girlfriend, being inappropriate, harassing you for your faith, etc., then request to be moved. It may be difficult to muster up the courage and say something, but it's worth it for the well-being of your soul and to have a great college experience. And in every situation, lead by example. Set the tone; don't react to it. The way you do – and do not – behave will speak volumes about who you are and whose you are. You belong to God.

> THE WAY YOU DO - AND DO NOT - BEHAVE WILL SPEAK VOLUMES ABOUT WHO YOU ARE AND WHOSE YOU ARE.

Coping with a Roommate:
Nobody's perfect. Everyone has faults and annoying habits. It's how you deal with those faults and annoying habits that will make you more tolerable as a roommate.

Here are some do's and don'ts:

DON'T:
- Gossip about your roommates, especially from one roommate to another.
- Be passive-aggressive or sarcastic ("Hmmm, I wonder who left these dirty dishes in the living room?!")
- Do anything you wouldn't want them to do to you.
- Pretend like you are perfect and without annoyances.
- Hold grudges.
- Let your roommates walk all over you.

DO:
- Be direct and honest about things that bother you (i.e, if their music is too loud, if they leave the bathroom messy, if they don't clean up after themselves).
- Offer solutions, rather than just mentioning problems.
- Create a cleaning schedule.
- Discuss what food you are okay with sharing, and what is yours.
- Compromise (bathroom time, TV time, who cooks what/when).
- Love people in their faults and weaknesses.

COMMUNITY

The people you surround yourself with in college is one of the most important factors in making your college experience wonderful and helping you grow in holiness. The people you spend the most time with influence who you are and what you do on the weekends, and they will either lead you closer to God or away from God. If you are going to a Catholic university, it will make finding people who share your faith a bit easier. If you are going to a secular university, it is still very possible to find good community, especially if there is a Catholic club on campus like FOCUS or a Newman Center.

Some of you may want to get involved in a Fraternity or Sorority to have community while in college. While there are some Fraternities and Sororities whose main focus is social outreach, academics, or

THE PEOPLE YOU SPEND THE MOST TIME WITH INFLUENCE WHO YOU ARE.

athletics, make sure that it is not outweighed by the party lifestyle that, while often portrayed to an extreme in the media, is nonetheless very real.

Even greater than the brotherhood or sisterhood that is found in Fraternities and Sororities is the family you have in Christ. Find a good young adult community that will affirm your faith and values, challenge you to live out the Gospel daily, and provide holy friendships. There are so many things you can do on weekends besides partying and getting drunk. Be creative and find fun things to do that will also allow your dignity to stay in tact.

Whether your freshman year – or your entire college career – is a fond memory or a painful wound depends, largely, on how you choose to spend your time and with whom you do so. Choose wisely.

CHAPTER THREE:
FINDING YOUR RHYTHM
BY NATALIE ALEMÁN AND CARRIE MILLER

It's easy to want to continue to live out your faith in college, but it's hard to actually do it. Yes, high school prepares you for what is to come – but you have to keep the momentum from what your youth minister was trying to hammer into you. Your faith will not come easy, Mass will not have the same music, and you will find yourself stuck in a paradox between two choices: will you live out your faith or not?

In high school your faith can be completely dependent on others without you ever realizing this. Was your prayer life marked simply by whatever your youth group was doing? People tend to not realize that they went to Mass to see their friends until they're not there anymore and they stop going. Aside from all the leadership conferences you may have gone to, witnesses you've given, and retreats you may have led, you will have to do things to ensure that your faith is sturdy before college and throughout it.

The foundation for your faith needs to be built on rock, rather than on sand (Matthew 7:26).

WHAT TO KNOW
Yes, a university faith environment is far different than a high school youth group. Your faith will be tested in ways that it wasn't before. Every time there is a period of transition, your faith will get rocked. Transitioning from high school youth group to college campus ministry is no different.

Campus ministry is not the same as youth

CAMPUS MINISTRY IS NOT THE SAME AS YOUTH MINISTRY.

13

ministry. At many universities, the Catholic student group is run like a club, complete with a president, faculty advisors, and fundraisers. That's completely different from what most of us experience in a high school youth group setting. But different is not necessarily a bad thing.

The focus of a high school youth group is often catechesis and spirituality – your youth minister wants to teach you about your faith and help you deepen your relationship with God.

The focus of a college campus ministry is similar – there is catechesis and spirituality, but most also have an emphasis on the new evangelization and formation. Yet, every campus's ministry will look different. Some will be focused primarily on fellowship – it's there so that Catholic students can meet and get to know other Catholic students. Others will have dynamic programs that are focused on conversion and formation. And unfortunately, there will be some universities that don't have any programs set up for Catholic students.

Regardless of how the program at your University is set up, you'll still have Mass and you'll still have all the Sacraments in any Catholic parish. You can make what you want out of any faith environment. So, even if the program is lacking or absent, you can find a community of faith if you look for it. It may not look the same as what you're used to, but be open to the different ways God wants to use you.

Another thing to keep in mind is that *youth* ministry is focused on *youth*. Your youth minister may have been able to call and "check in" with you if they noticed you missed Mass. A campus minister will not do that. Your campus minister is going to expect that you're making decisions for yourself.

It's not that a campus minister doesn't care about you; it means that they expect you to act like an adult and make decisions for yourself (growing up is a double edged sword). That will determine where your faith really is, whether it's based on Christ or on others. But, there are things that you can do before the training wheels come off to ensure that your faith will remain primary.

KNOW YOURSELF
Know who you are and who God made you to be. Your identity in

Him is the most important thing to keep in mind. You are made in His image and likeness (Genesis 1:27). To know yourself, you have to know who God is.

God is consistent and unchanging. What are the things that are unchanging in your life? The things that are unchanging are the things that will help you make sense of change.

Know what's important to you. What are your non-negotiables? Make a list of them. Write it down if you have to. Is it that you want to make sure you are going to Sunday Mass? Daily Mass? Daily prayer? Write down your commitments; these are the things that you know make you who you are, who you want to be, and who God made you to be. Do whatever it takes to live out your identity as a beloved son or daughter of God.

KNOW WHAT'S IMPORTANT TO YOU. WHAT ARE YOUR NON-NEGOTIABLES?

It is vital to stay true to yourself. God created you in a specific way, with specific gifts, talents, and preferences. If you stay true to the person God created you to be, the transition from high school to college – especially for your faith – will be much smoother.

ESTABLISH A FOUNDATION

A foundation in your faith is necessary for success. The rock is much firmer and stronger than sand (Matthew 7:25-27). There are things that, regardless of where you are, will help you keep your faith.

Your foundation has to be on Christ and the things that point toward Him, and it's important that you seek out the things that will build on your foundation.

Community

Even, the earliest Christians made sure they had a community that could support their specific needs (Acts 2:42). Two thousand years later, a community is just as necessary. There hopefully is a community of Catholic students at your university. At some schools, it's called the

Newman Center. At others, it might be called the Catholic Student Union or Catholic Center. Regardless of the name, the purpose is usually the same.

At the beginning of the fall semester, every club on campus recruits for new members and tries to spread the word about fun events they have coming up. The Catholic organization will be no different. They'll have some fun start-of-the-year events, like an opening BBQ or a Welcome Mass. Some even go to great lengths to ensure that freshmen feel welcome with dorm visits by older students and personal calls to invite. The Catholic clubs gain nothing from you joining, it's not like there are dues that they want paid; they simply want you to be a part of their community. They want you to feel welcome on campus and desire that you have a place to live out your faith. Go to the events, because you'll be able to meet other freshmen that don't know anybody else either, as well as some awesome people who already know their way around the campus, the town, and the church.

Most Catholic student centers also have a student Mass each Sunday that's usually later in the day, similar to the Life Teen mass you're used to in that it's geared toward a specific age group. The music will be different, the lectors may be older, and you'll probably find yourself comparing the Mass to the Mass you're used to. Do your best to remind yourself that it's Jesus that you are there for, not the music or the people. You'll find that you'll come to love this new Mass for different reasons than you love the Life Teen Mass; and that is okay.

Most campus ministry programs have a night, similar to a Life Night, that happens once a week. Get their calendar and jot down the events they have throughout the month. There are Bible studies, discernment groups, Newman nights, socials, praise and worship, holy hours, service opportunities, intra-mural sports teams, and almost anything you can think of. Catholic campus ministry programs are robust and dynamic enough that you can find anything you're interested in there. If not, it's a great place to find students who want to start up similar types of groups.

What's more, though, is that not only will you have friends to join you at Mass and other events, you'll also have people to pray for you and with you. It's impossible to overemphasize how important this is. There will come a day when having a prayerful community to support you will be a necessity, especially when you're feeling homesick or stressed (we've all had those days!).

For those of you who may find yourself at a university that does not have a program for Catholic students, finding a community can be a bit harder. Find a parish near your university that you become involved in. There may be one with an active youth ministry program that you can be a Core Member at, or there may be others that have young adult programs that you can join. Don't think that finding a community is hopeless; it just may take more work to find one.

THERE WILL COME A DAY WHEN HAVING A PRAYERFUL COMMUNITY TO SUPPORT YOU WILL BE A NECESSITY.

Develop a Rhythm of Prayer

"Prayer doesn't help your relationship with God. It is your relationship with God." This is a quote I've heard over and over, and its truth hits me every time. Being away from family for the first time is challenging. Getting used to a new school and new people and new everything is challenging. But God is constant, no matter where you go or what your campus ministry is like.

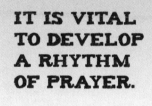

IT IS VITAL TO DEVELOP A RHYTHM OF PRAYER.

It is vital to develop a rhythm of prayer. Notice that I say "rhythm of prayer," not just "have a prayer life." There is a difference. For most of my college career, my prayer life consisted of Mass on Sunday and then begging God for help when I was stressed out because of school or felt completely alone and unsupported by the people I had surrounded myself with. I had a prayer life. I talked to God. But I did not have a rhythm of prayer. My prayer life was based on whether things were going well in the rest of my life or if I wanted something, not on an irreplaceable relationship with the God of my heart.

A rhythm of prayer is important because it does not change. It's ok to start small. In fact, it's probably better to pray every morning for ten or fifteen minutes at 8:30 than to pray for an hour whenever you can throughout a particular day. Why? Because, as humans, we respond best to structure. Even if it feels like you're doing all the talking in those fifteen minutes, if you're faithful to a rhythm of prayer, you'll soon see how God is moving in your life throughout the day. You'll soon understand how God communicates with you. You'll be able to discern God's will for you more easily when you're intimately connected with him through prayer.

When you have a rhythm of prayer, talking to God isn't just something you do when you need help; it becomes a true relationship. Eventually, you'll find that you want more and more time with God. Take it! Build prayer time into your daily schedule, because it is only through our connection with God that we find the strength to boldly live a genuine Catholic lifestyle.

Keep in Mind...
This might seem like a very obvious statement, but the layout of the church at your school's Catholic Center will be different from the layout of your church at home. Ask for a tour so that you can be as comfortable there as possible, so when it's time to go to an event by yourself, you already know where the students hang out, or where the confessional is, or where daily Mass is celebrated.

Also, give it time. The Catholic group is designed to help meet the needs of college students, so while it might be a tough transition, don't forget that you spent years developing your relationships at your home parish. Those kinds of relationships can't be developed overnight! Try your Newman Center for at least one semester, and if you're still not clicking with it, then don't be afraid to start new things.

Make the community what you want it to be. If you love Bible studies and there isn't one being offered, talk to your campus ministers about possibly starting one. They can point you to resources to help guide you and they'll probably point you towards other students that can do it with you. More than likely the ministry has a mission and if you don't understand it, don't be afraid to see what you can do to help it be a more fully alive community.

REINFORCE YOUR FOUNDATION… AND BUILD ON IT

The Church has provided us with an amazing wealth of resources to take our journey of faith to the next level. Among them are big things like Sacraments, Mass, Adoration, patron saints, and written resources like prayers and books.

Sacraments

Be greedy with the Sacraments. They are the best way to stay in God's grace. Make sure you're going to Sunday Mass, of course, but also go to weekday Mass when your schedule permits. The Eucharist is the source and summit of all we do and all we are as Catholics, so take any opportunity you can to receive Christ.

Frequent the confessional. The best way to remain united with God is through the Sacrament of Reconciliation. Receiving God's grace in this way can transform your life.

Adoration

The second-best thing you can do to strengthen your foundation and your intimacy with God is to sit in silence with our Lord before the

FREQUENT THE CONFESSIONAL.

Blessed Sacrament. Your Newman Center may not have a perpetual Adoration chapel, but another church in the area probably will. Once your daily prayer rhythm is established, take some time to visit an Adoration chapel at least once a week.

Prayers

Don't be afraid to supplement your daily prayer with particular devotions, such as the Rosary or Chaplet of Divine Mercy. Another great resource is Liturgy of the Hours. The Liturgy of the Hours is the Church's second-highest form of prayer, second only to the Mass. It's basically a book of psalms and readings broken up into a four-week cycle, with different psalms for different times of the day (Morning, Mid-Morning, Noon, Afternoon, Evening, and Night). It is a great way to stay rooted in Scripture and because of how it's set up, it enhances a rhythm of prayer.

Spiritual Reading

The saints of the Catholic Church provide invaluable insight and wisdom for a bold Christian life. If you have a saint you love or have a special connection with, check out any of their writings.

There are a ton of other resources out there, too. Check out authors like Scott Hahn, Peter Kreeft, and C.S. Lewis (Lewis isn't Catholic but his writings on Christianity are great).

Spiritual Direction

Spiritual direction is another great resource. It provides the opportunity to journey with another person in your faith. It typically involves sharing what's happening in your life and prayer life, and allowing the other person (often a priest or trained spiritual director) to give insight and direction. A spiritual director might suggest certain Scripture passages to pray through, or offer guidance in other areas of your life, like physical exercise and sleep.

SPIRITUAL DIRECTION IS ANOTHER GREAT RESOURCE.

The biggest change (and challenge) you'll encounter is taking full ownership of your faith once you get to college. Know who God is. Know who you are. Know where to find the community and resources you'll need to transition successfully from your high school youth group to your college faith environment.

COLLEGE PREP

BY MARK HART

Here are some things that you should take some time to figure out before you get to college:

☐ **Define what your goal is for college.** Actually write it out on paper. While you're at it, write out the limits you want to place on your social life, your sexuality, and your morality. Set parameters for yourself. Draw lines in the sand that you will not cross for anyone, and then have the courage to stick by them. The great Catholic author G.K. Chesterton once said,

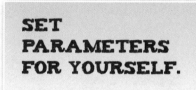

SET PARAMETERS FOR YOURSELF.

"Morality, like art, begins with drawing a line somewhere."

☐ **Invite someone to walk your collegiate faith walk with you.** This should be someone there on campus (not just back home). Invite them to hold you accountable to go to church. Ask them to pray with you regularly. Give them permission to call you out if you get lazy or if they see you start to drift morally. Do the same for them. There's a reason Jesus sent the apostles out two by two. There's strength in numbers. Remember, "where two or three are gathered in (Christ's) Name…there He is in their midst" (Matthew 18:20).

☐ **Stay mindful of how blessed you are.** Many of the souls you'll encounter in college didn't have what you had in terms of family or a youth group or just openness to God and knowledge of His love for you. If those who supposedly "know" Jesus don't act like it, where is the hope for the rest who haven't been blessed like you have? That doesn't

PEOPLE SHOULD SEE HOPE IN YOU.

mean your life has been easy or that it will be. It means that you are God's billboard on campus. People should see hope in you – and when they see it, they'll come asking you where it comes from (1 Peter 3:15). Remember your responsibility, guard your example, and be prepared to share your testimony.

☐ **Rediscover the lost art of conversation.** In this screen-based culture, people are becoming increasingly socially inept. It's more about "what I have to say" (or text, or blog, or post, or tweet) than what others are trying to say to me. Don't be one of those people. Ask questions that penetrate the heart. Affirm in ways that stir the soul. Make eye contact with those across from you. Seek Christ in the other. The Holy Spirit will give you the words if you give Him your heart and ask Him to guide you to the souls who most need Christ in you.

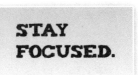

STAY FOCUSED.

☐ **Stay focused.** There will always be "something else to do." There will always be someone heading out on a Wednesday night. There will always be someone wanting to avoid homework on the random Tuesday or wanting to distract you on the mundane Thursday. Stay focused. The sooner you get the other things done and the more disciplined you can stay with your workload, the more relaxed, successful, and joyful you will remain. The devil offers distractions; God offers solutions.

NEVER SACRIFICE YOUR DIGNITY ON AN ALTAR OF CONFORMITY AND PUBLIC OPINION.

☐ **Keep your eyes on the prize.** The prize at the end of your time in college is not a degree, a job, funny stories, or a lifelong social network… those things might be there, but they are not the end goal. The end goal – even beyond your heightened social skill set, your emotional maturity, and your sharpened intellect – is your sainthood. Never sacrifice your dignity on an altar of conformity and public opinion. People may not agree with your pursuit of sanctity – they might even mock it (Matthew 5:10-11) – but they will respect it; and respect cannot be bought or negotiated, it is won.

College has the potential to be the greatest experience of your life or the fastest route to spiritual death. The choice is in your hands.

Choose wisely

FORWARD
THINKING

FORWARD THINKING

While working on this resource, we realized that a typical college student will go through various situations within the next couple years. From breakups to failed exams, to financial issues all the way to decorating a new room—you will encounter a bunch of new things. In order to address that, this part of the book is different than the previous part. Numerous authors have contributed to this portion of the book. They share their personal experiences on specific topics or issues that you may face while in college.

The Forward Thinking section is designed so you can look up a specific topic and read a short piece with practical tips and information. These are meant to be general guidelines to help you throughout your college career. They are not written to address everything that has to do with a specific topic, but they are fun, informative overviews. The way you apply each to your life will differ depending on your background, major, or university. But our hope is that these sections will be there when you need solid advice, or simply when you need a reminder that you're not the only one who may be going through something.

You are the only one that can determine how your college life looks, and we hope that you feel encouraged by all of us within the movement of Life Teen.

ABUSE

Whether you're not sure if you or a friend is being abused, or you're very sure, here are some of the things you need to know.

Before anything else, you need to know first of all that every person is loved, not only by God but also by countless people who are longing to help those stuck in abusive relationships. No one deserves to be treated this way. You can know that deep down, but the thing about abuse is that for some reason, the abuser makes you believe you deserve to be treated this way.

NO ONE DESERVES TO BE TREATED THIS WAY.

Do not be afraid. If you are being abused you have to believe that you were made for more and you don't have to put up with it. Someone who is abusive thrives off of the silence of the one they are abusing. They will use threats, manipulation, and whatever else works to try to keep you from exposing them.

The word abuse means to use in the wrong way, or to mistreat. Physical abuse is the mistreatment of your body. Emotional abuse is the mistreating of your emotions. Someone is emotionally abusive if they are controlling, manipulative, or will ostracize you or "withdraw" and act distant if you don't do what they want, agree with them, or say what they want. Sexual abuse is the mistreatment of your own free will in your sexuality, either through force or manipulation. Verbal abuse is to be attacked verbally and torn down for who you are or what you do.

YOU DESERVE TO BE RESPECTED, LOVED, AND CARED FOR NO MATTER WHAT.

Each kind of abuse is an offense against your inherent dignity as a person. You deserve to be respected, loved, and cared for no matter what.

It's common to be afraid to tell others what's going on. You might be afraid that people will think less of you, or that the abuse will get worse. Your campus health center will have plenty of resources to help you out. There are also phone numbers you can call anonymously to talk to someone about it.

Lastly, don't despair and give up hope. Healing is possible and a totally new life awaits you.

ALCOHOL ABUSE

You may be away from home for the very first time and relishing the freedom that being away at college provides. There's no one looking over your shoulder, asking who you're with, what you're doing, if you've finished your homework, or what time you're coming home.

While heading off to college is a wonderful opportunity to really grow in maturity and responsibility, when combined with the availability of easily obtainable and cheap alcohol, the temptation to partake and/or overindulge can be hard to resist.

Besides not being a good idea on any level, giving in to underage and excessive drinking can bring the following unexpected and unwanted results:

A Criminal Record

While it may seem like "everyone" does it or that it's no big deal, underage drinking is in fact a crime that, if you're 18 or older, will be a part of your permanent history. If you've used a forged ID to obtain the alcohol you can also be charged with that offense as well, or with a DUI if you get behind the wheel.

With lowered inhibitions, you also put yourself at risk of doing things you wouldn't ordinarily do. Disorderly conduct, property damage, noise violations, and assaults are frequently associated with the college-drinking scene. If you commit any of these alcohol related crimes, every time you apply for a job those youthful indiscretions will rear their ugly heads and may cost you a job that you really want.

WITH LOWERED INHIBITIONS, YOU ALSO PUT YOURSELF AT RISK OF DOING THINGS YOU WOULDN'T ORDINARILY DO.

Engaging in Sexual Activity

Being on your own and away from home provides many opportunities – and temptations – to be alone with that "special someone." You may have the best of intentions to live chastely, but with the lowered inhibitions that alcohol consumption brings, you could very easily give in to the moment and end up regretting your actions. You also place yourself at risk of the advances of "not so special someones" who could quickly take advantage of your lowered resistance.

Injury or Death

At the start of every school year one has only to open the newspapers to read the alcohol related tragedy du jour. Under the influence of alcohol, students have fallen out of windows and off balconies, stepped in front of cars, perished in traffic accidents, been raped, kidnapped and/or succumbed to alcohol poisoning. While this all sounds quite dramatic, sadly, it happens. Under the influence of alcohol your judgment is impaired, inhibitions all but eliminated, and reason squashed.

With all the potential pitfalls and dangers associated with underage and excessive drinking, just stay safe and stay away.

ACADEMICS

Imagine arriving to your very first college class. You may be feeling excited and nervous, and hopefully you aren't late. Now imagine opening up the door to your classroom and seeing 300 other students already seated and waiting for class to begin.

This is called a "lecture hall."

And it's just one of many things that make a college class different from the classes you took in high school. These kinds of changes can seem intimidating, but if you can adjust to these differences you will be much happier and less stressed. Failure to adjust may result in you curling into fetal position in the corner of the classroom. It makes taking notes inconvenient, and it's an awful way to make new friends.

The first difference is that "the teaching style changes." Professors are going to talk through the entire class and expect you to take notes – say goodbye to using class time for homework. You can adjust to this change by sharpening your note taking skills. Make up abbreviations for commonly used terms so you don't have to write them out, and be selective about what you write in your notebook. You don't need to take notes on the story your professor told about their last golf game. If possible, meet with other students in the class once per week to compare notes, and make sure there isn't anything you've missed.

Second, there is a lot more reading required for your college courses and the professor doesn't necessarily check to see if you have completed it. Don't let yourself get behind on reading. Make and stick to a schedule for completing your reading assignments before each class. It will help you understand your lectures, and eliminate the need to "cram" before a test.

Third, professors are rarely available after class for questions. Every professor has "office hours"; these times are specifically set-aside for him or her to meet with students and answer questions face to face. Learn your professor's office hours and make use of them.

Remember to make these adjustments early. By adjusting to the changes right away you will find you are less stressed and you get much better grades. One last bit of advice – get to class early; finding a seat among 300 people can be a lot trickier than you think.

ACCOUNTABILITY

Staying grounded and rooted in faith during college is tough. Whether you are looking for them or not, distractions and temptations will find you when you get to college. No matter where you are on your faith journey, the path to virtue and holiness will require someone to walk with you to keep you focused and accountable to what really matters, specifically in the areas of morals and faith.

Here are a few steps to take when setting up accountability in your life:

1. **Find someone to hold you accountable.** The person you choose to keep you accountable should be someone who you feel has a solid foundation of faith. This person can be a friend at the same college, your youth minister, a Core Member, parish priest, spiritual director, or a campus minister. The person you choose should know you well and be someone you look up to and respect. Ask that person if they can commit to helping you stay accountable to holiness and that they would be praying for you.

2. **Make a list of commitments.** Take some time to pray and think about what things you may need help staying accountable to during college. Is it going to Mass on Sundays? Is it a regular routine of Confession? Is it daily prayer? Is it going to class every day and studying? Is it finding new community? Is it staying away from drinking and partying? Is it staying pure? Whatever your list looks like, write it down and give a copy to your accountability partner.

3. **Talk or meet with your accountability partner regularly.** Set up weekly or monthly times to talk or meet with your accountability partner. This is a time for you to share how you are doing and what you need prayers for. It also gives your accountability partner a chance to ask about your commitments. Be honest about what's going on in your life and listen to what your partner has to say.

> **THERE IS GRACE IN TRIAL.**

One last thing – expect that this won't be easy. It will require discipline, honesty, balance, and commitment. When it gets hard or you feel like you've failed, don't give up. There is grace in trial. Just ask St. Paul (Romans 8:18, 2 Corinthians 12:9).

ADDICTION

Addiction is not something anyone plans on. It is not a life goal. You have probably already decided against having one (if you have not made that decision it might be a good time to go ahead and do so). But it might not be as simple as just saying "No, thank you." Addiction typically does not ask your permission. It is much more subtle than that. It may start out as a couple drinks at a party. "Well, a lot of people do that. Does mean that they are alcoholics?" What makes one person an addict and another not?

> **ADDICTION TYPICALLY DOES NOT ASK YOUR PERMISSION.**

Addiction is more than a habit. It when your brain processes things in a way that makes the desire for your addiction so great that it outweighs the related consequences. You may tell yourself that an addiction is not a big deal when all the evidence points to another obvious conclusion, or you may know it is problem and not be able to stop.

Classically, addiction has been thought of as a substance abuse issue, but more and more the evidence points to a much broader understanding. Addictions range from drug addiction to media addiction (constant connection via smart phones). The story of a college freshman who flunks out because he spent hours on X-box live is not that uncommon.

Some common college addictions include:

- Porn addictions
- Drug addictions
- Alcoholism
- Gaming addictions
- Gambling addictions

Lists like this are never sufficient and chances are you will encounter something that is not on the list. But then again, there is a very good chance you will encounter these exact things. You may not be addicted yourself, but, statistically speaking, you will know someone who is.

So, how do you know if you have an addiction? Well, if you find yourself asking the question "Am I addicted?" it is a good indication you might be. Another thing to consider is: have you noticed any behaviors or habits that are getting in the way of your relationships or responsibilities? Do you find yourself losing control of the situation? Have you ever lied about it? Have you tried to stop? If you are nodding your head you might have a problem.

RECOVERY IS NOT A ONE-DAY THING. IT IS A LIFETIME THING.

So, what if you do have an addiction? You need to know that it is a big deal, bigger than you can handle on your own. It sounds like a cliché, but just admitting you might have a problem is a big step towards dealing with it. The next step is admitting you need help and getting that help – help from other people, and help from God. Your campus probably has a counseling center or medical office. This is a great place to start your walk to recovery. Your campus probably also has a Newman club or Catholic organization. That is another great place to go for help. Talk to your priest, or campus minister. This is not an either or thing. Do both. Remember, recovery is not a one-day thing. It is a lifetime thing. The sooner you start, the better the rest of that lifetime will be.

BALANCE

The average schedules for college students are an obnoxious mix of: class time, gross amounts of studying, carb-heavy work hours, a small assortment of both family and friend time, and *lastly,* a side of Christ. More than likely your senior year of high school looked nothing like this. But college is known to make your balanced "time diet" quickly become unbalanced and overweight in one semester. How could this happen?

Answer: it's easy, as a "noob" (new inexperienced person) to the college scene, to show little respect for the syllabus. Each professor hands out a syllabus at the beginning of the semester and it contains ALL test dates, project deadlines, paper deadlines – basically, anything that you are responsible to turn in for that particular course.

Always remember, your primary responsibility is to be a successful student and those syllabi will definitely start you off on the right track.

By using your syllabus to see how your semesters will pan out in ALL your courses, you're able to:

- Eliminate surprise due dates.
- Set manageable goals for completing projects.
- Estimate where you should be academically within the semester.
- Efficiently allocate time to study, hang with friends/family, rest, work, and spend time with God.

At this point in your life, your time commitments have shifted, and the faster you can adapt, the better off you'll be. One of the best practices you could implement with scheduling is a time budget. In the beginning you'll keep track of the amount of time spent doing everything throughout the day, and I mean *everything*.

Your track sheet could include:

- Getting ready for class
- Copying notes from a friend

- Waiting in lines for food or coffee
- Making your way around campus
- Time spent on social websites
- Time for God
- General class time

Take time to record where you spend all your time. For example, if you need more time in-between lunch and class to study for an exam, based off your track sheets you'll figure out what food places took the least amount of time to get to, order, and get out so you could get back to studying quickly.

INSTEAD OF SPENDING LESS TIME WITH GOD AND AT SOCIAL GATHERINGS, YOU'LL ACTUALLY BE SPENDING LESS TIME WASTING TIME.

This might sound nerdy, but you'll be a lean, time-saving machine in no time. Instead of spending less time with God and at social gatherings, you'll actually be spending less time wasting time.

Like any normal human, becoming unhealthy doesn't happen overnight. As you learn how to manage time, the glaring "fatty" areas of your life that tip the scales will become apparent. This is a good thing because you'll quickly put those on a diet, adding muscle to areas in your life that really count.

BREAKUPS

Relationships are hard, but breakups are harder. If you've ever been through a breakup, or are going through one, it can be easy to feel like no one will be able to take his or her place. There is no way around the fact that they're hard.

Of course, it doesn't hit you until everything in your heart aches for their company. Memories of them fill your mind, and it's tough to imagine that they're actually gone. It's especially harder when your identity has been placed in the relationship. When it's gone, it's a struggle to put your identity back to where it belongs, with Christ.

Breakups are never easy, even if you're the one who has initiated the split. You feel as if the memories can't be escaped and you find yourself constantly questioning whether or not you're doing the right thing. It can be easy to try to relive the relationship in your mind, hoping to figure out what exactly went wrong. But, the reality is that the past is frozen and as hard as it is, you have to be in the present.

You may find yourself afraid of being alone or feeling lonely. To desperately try to escape the pain, it can be easy to try to jump at any person who comes your way. Don't try to convince yourself that they are not a "rebound." The reality is that you can't move forward into another relationship if your heart clings to another person. You have to be healed first from the hurt prior to entering into a new relationship, especially if it's going to be a healthy relationship.

You need time; time to be you, time to be single…truly single. Time to truly set yourself free from the hurt, time to feel your pain, take it in, and give it to God. Time is necessary to letting the hole in your heart heal with the grace of God. Letting Him take it, repair it, and fill it.

The memories may come, but know that it gets easier with His grace. Know that

TIME IS NECESSARY TO HEAL WITH THE GRACE OF GOD.

this pain is not forever and that one day it will also become a memory. The God who loves you will help you, but only if you let Him. Trust that He will bring the right person for you, if you're called to marriage, in His perfect timing. Be comfortable waiting on the Lord— He is always faithful.

Here are some tangible ways to help deal with a breakup:

- **Time:** Let the pain you have heal. It takes time.

- **Pray:** Ask Him to heal you, to heal the wounds in your heart and shine light into the areas that hurt.

- **Trust:** Ask the Lord for the grace to trust His will for you. The grace to trust that He has someone that will exceed your expectations.

- **Grow:** Give yourself time to be you. Give yourself time to be you. Get to know yourself; your strength, your weaknesses, and your desires. "Become who you are" (Blessed John Paul II).

CAMPUS MINISTRY

Walking into an "Involvement Fair" for the first time may leave you a little overwhelmed. Picture it: thousands of students on a lawn area and just about the same amount of clubs and organizations all vying for your attention. While it's true that you'll receive a year's supply of free food and logo gifts that day, knowing how to get involved will be a little unclear. At many schools, choosing a campus ministry program is similar: multiple Catholic groups, service groups, Christian groups, and the list goes on. Not to worry! If you know what you are going into, and know your goals, the process of getting involved in campus ministry can be smooth and even enjoyable.

Use these steps as some guidelines to get started:

1. **It is going to look different.** The whole structure of college, church, and ministry is different. You may feel frustrated and disappointed because you miss your old faith community.

2. **Get involved, somehow.** You are meant to be in community with other Catholics, and you are meant to grow in holiness. Don't fall into the trap of thinking you can be active in your faith on your own. Jesus and His disciples were in community to model this to us.

3. **More options than you think.** The beautiful thing about college is that it gives you a lot of different options. Pick the ministry that fits you best and invest in that one. Being active in one ministry is always better than just being present in several.

4. **Lead the change.** You may not like certain aspects of your campus ministry program. But what if you are

> **DON'T FALL INTO THE TRAP OF THINKING YOU CAN BE ACTIVE IN YOUR FAITH ON YOUR OWN.**

called to change those aspects or introduce new ones? Can you imagine the impact of introducing Adoration or a Bible study to your campus group? What about a mission trip? God may be calling you to this.

5. **Focus on what matters.** Sure, the social time is great. I love a good spaghetti dinner too. But remember the reason for campus ministry in the first place. Leading your campus closer to Christ is always the mission. As you get involved and make decisions, keep this mission in the forefront of your thoughts.

For years, high school students have been known to go to college and lose their faith. But you're part of a generation of college students who are rising up and taking their faith to the next level. If you partner with campus ministry to do this, imagine the impact!

CAMPUS INVOLVEMENT

College provides many opportunities for you to be involved in numerous types of clubs or groups – anything from the Catholic Center, to community service groups, to fraternities and sororities. There are intramural sports, performing arts, and specialized groups dedicated to a cause. Most campuses have hundreds of clubs or groups. The possibilities are endless! Deciding what to get involved with can be a little overwhelming. Where do you even start?

Start first by determining how much time you can commit to a club or group. Look at your schedule for the semester. How many hours are you taking? Do you have enough time to give to something new? The key to successful involvement is balancing your time.

> **THE KEY TO SUCCESSFUL INVOLVEMENT IS BALANCING YOUR TIME.**

Second, decide what you are interested in. Is it community service? Is it particular to your major? Is it a cause like AIDS or Right to Life? If you have an undeclared major, finding a club or group that focuses on your interests can hopefully help you make a decision about what you might major in.

Third, narrow down the clubs or groups by doing some research to see what your school has available. Talk to the people in your classes or dorm to find out what they are involved in. Find a couple of clubs or groups that interest you and seek out more information.

Finally, go to a meeting. Most clubs or groups (with the exception of some fraternities and sororities) will host information meetings during the first few weeks of the year. Find out when they are and go.

In your research you may find that there is not an existing club or group for your particular interest. If that's the case, start one! You'll probably be able to find more people who have the same interest as you.

If you are not interested in joining a specific club or group but still desire to be involved, look into campus-wide events. If your college has a sports program, go to the games and cheer on the team. Participate in pep rallies prior to the games.

Check at your student union for events like carnivals or socials happening around campus. Is your dorm hosting an event? Sign up and participate.

In all of this, remember that the key to a successful college life is to stay balanced and focused. Keep all these things in mind when choosing what to get involved in while at school.

CHASTITY

Now that you are in college, whether you are living at home or in a dorm, there is a newfound freedom. Especially if you are living in a dorm, your curfew may be very different than when you were at home.

How does this translate to chastity? Now that you are in college, it's up to you to define your boundaries. It is not impossible to stay chaste while in college. Yes, the world will throw everything your way to make you believe that sex in college is inevitable. But, the truth is, you can remain chaste in college! You just need the right tools.

First, if you are in a dating relationship, have a talk with your boy/girlfriend and together define boundaries that will lead you both to holiness. Don't wait until you are in the moment. If you struggle with talking about sex and sexuality with your boy/girlfriend, then reconsider if he/she is the one you should be dating. The other part of this is the "hooking up" trap. Media would have you believe that no one in college dates anymore – they are merely hooking up. Hold fast to your convictions!

Second, it's Friday night, your roommate is gone, and you are broke. The local $1 movie rental and the convenience of your dorm room seems the logical choice for a date. So many things can go wrong here! Lying in bed together, snuggled tightly, and "nodding" off isn't chastity – especially when it becomes a habit and you are sleeping through the night together. Chastity isn't just about physical purity – it's about purity of heart, mind, and soul. Decide to protect each other's chastity and keep your dates public. You can still find inexpensive things to do that won't end up in a darkened dorm room.

> **CHASTITY ISN'T JUST ABOUT PHYSICAL PURITY – IT'S ABOUT PURITY OF HEART, MIND, AND SOUL.**

Third, you need to develop a community of support. Trying to navigate all of the pressures and temptations of college life on your own can be very difficult. So don't do it alone. Find the local Newman Center and get involved. When you were in high school you may have felt the support of your youth group, your youth minister, or even your pastor. Seek out people who are striving to live the same way that you are and be willing to share your struggles and ask for support and accountability.

Lastly, if you haven't read anything about Theology of the Body, now would be a good time to start. The best place to start is with the book *Theology of the Body for Beginners* by Christopher West. In between studying for class, take some time to go to a chapel, read a chapter, and ask for the intercession of Mary and St. Joseph!

CHEATING

By the time you enter college, you have already been presented with the opportunity to cheat and have been pressured to do so. Sadly this is a common occurrence in high schools, colleges, and universities. As you move up the educational ladder, each year proves more challenging than the first. Getting a degree requires hard work and dedication, and college proves to be the most thought-provoking time in your life.

As the classwork piles on, the pressure to get assignments finished increases, and stresses build – the idea of cheating becomes appealing. This is a very normal feeling to have. You will feel pressure; college isn't easy. Cheating is simply taking the work of another person and claiming it to be your own. You may feel like you have no control over the craze your life has become and that you can no longer manage your studies – but you can.

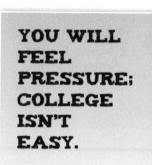

YOU WILL FEEL PRESSURE; COLLEGE ISN'T EASY.

We must refrain from the temptation to cheat. We have been taught from the beginning that cheating is wrong, and it is evident within the seventh commandment: "thou shall not steal." But what are we to do when the going gets tough? Did Jesus ask anyone else to take His place on the cross? There are alternative ways to handle these temptations rather than cheating.

Here are some things you can do to avoid cheating:

1. **Pray.** Jesus tells us that we can do all things through Him and that He'll never give us anything that we are not able to handle. You're here for a reason; ask Him for the grace to finish your assignments.

2. **Have someone hold you accountable.** Instead of turning to cheating, tell someone what you're struggling with. Ask them to hold you responsible for maintaining your academic

integrity. Whenever you feel tempted to cheat, simply call your accountability partner and ask for his/her help.

3. **Ask Questions.** Stay in constant communication with your professors and establish a good relationship with them. At the first sign of not understanding a concept, ask questions. And when all else fails and you feel like nothing is helping, go to the on-campus tutors. Tutors are very beneficial and can help you to stay on track.

Also remember: the negative stereotype, "once a cheater, always a cheater," could not be farther from the truth. We can change our lives around, seek help in our mistakes, and ask the Lord to lead us. Think of how much more you'll learn if *you* put in the work for your major rather than using the work of someone else.

Do not lose hope, just stay focused and keep your priorities straight. God loves you despite your imperfections. He has created you with the ability to do all things through Him. He wants to see what you can do, not what others can do for you. He loves you and the work *you* do.

CLASSES

College is an exciting time in life: independence, meeting new people, fun, and classes. Wait, what? Classes? Yes, in the midst of all your newfound freedom there is one requirement: you actually have to take classes. Here are some tips to help you engage in all of your classes (the good ones and the bad):

Registering for Classes

Unlike in high school where your schedule was basically assigned to you, in college you choose your own classes. Not only is this pretty cool, but it also offers you a lot of freedom. If your university allows you to pre-register, be sure to take advantage of the opportunity. While you may not get all the classes you requested, you'll be a lot better off than those who wait until the last minute. If, on the other hand, your college does not offer pre-registration, be sure to plan ahead by researching the classes and times they are offered. Remember, if you aren't properly prepared and a class fills up, you could miss out on one that you really want or need to take.

Take the Hard Class

College offers a lot of options in terms of classes. In many ways, you'll be tempted to take the easy way out. Before you fill up your schedule with classes like underwater basket weaving, the art of walking, or one about your favorite superheroes, try taking classes that will challenge you. Here are a couple recommendations that are not only good for most majors but also for most jobs after college: public speaking, marketing, or accounting.

Show Up

One of the most tempting things to do in college is to skip class. While in high school this would have resulted in an express trip to detention, college does not work like that. Teachers are there to teach, and students are there to learn. When you skip

TEACHERS ARE THERE TO TEACH, AND STUDENTS ARE THERE TO LEARN.

a class, you miss an opportunity to learn something that could benefit your future. On top of this, you (or your parents) are paying *a lot* of money for this education, so if you don't show up to class, the only person you're hurting is you.

Participate

Do you want to know the easiest way to make a class more enjoyable? Participate. By participating in class discussions, taking notes, or asking questions, you are not only taking a proactive role in your education, but you may give your fellow classmates an opportunity to learn from someone other than the professor. As an added bonus, your professor will also get to know you better, which can only benefit you when it's time to assign grades.

COMMUNITY

The faith that we live must be personal, but it cannot be entirely individual. Just as you need a foundation of faith in your life, you also need a foundation of friends, family, and a community to support you. And what better way to grow in holiness than by finding peers who are also striving for holiness?

College is a growing experience, and regarding community, that means that it's going to be your job to seek it out. In high school, your community may have come very easily. You may have made friends naturally, or already had some old friends and built your own community. But now that you're in college you're going to have to work at getting into a community, and that's going to take perseverance and patience. But don't worry; this is not an impossible task. The real question you should ask yourself is, what do you look for in a community, and why should you even look for it?

> **YOU'RE GOING TO HAVE TO WORK AT GETTING INTO A COMMUNITY.**

You should look for community because trying to live a faithful life by yourself is a losing battle. College is a journey that you embark on, away from home, where 92.3% of the time, you will need to make your own decisions, including the decision to seek community.

You need a community to pray with, serve with, and even laugh with. But amazing, beautiful people who call you to holiness aren't just going to show up at your dorm room. And sure, you might be able to find good friends around campus, but take into consideration that you might need to start up your own community. Whether it's five of your friends or a group of twenty people, if you're comfortable around them and they make you a better person, then you're doing something right.

So don't undergo the perilous adventure of college alone, but find some friends who call you to be a better person. Those are the people that will call you to holiness. And good friends can be found almost anywhere in college. Whether it's in your classes, your dorm, your Newman Center, or your psychology club, there are plenty of opportunities for you to find healthy friendships all over your new college campus.

DECORATING YOUR ROOM

Whether it's a stack of unopened textbooks that function as a nightstand, or it's a perpetual hamper explosion, college rooms take on a variety of looks. The lackluster appearance of a blank white wall and extra long twin size beds will remain as a perpetual reminder that this is foreign territory until you start to decorate.

How you decorate your new place says a lot about who you are, where you're from, and what you find valuable. It can say good things about you. If sports play a significant role in your life, fill your room with items that fit that passion. If you love polka dots and paisley, buy sheets, frames, and throw pillows to reflect that. If your faith has been important to you, don't hesitate putting up a crucifix. Fearing what others will think can't influence your decision to put something on your wall, especially if it's something important to you.

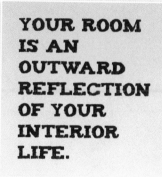

YOUR ROOM IS AN OUTWARD REFLECTION OF YOUR INTERIOR LIFE.

A word of caution: the way you decorate your room can also reveal negative things about you. There is nothing more embarrassing for a woman than when she walks into a guy's room and sees images of scantily clad women plastered everywhere. That doesn't impress a woman; in fact, it does quite the opposite.

Your room is an outward reflection of your interior life – the phrase "if walls could talk" really has a deeper meaning; don't take it lightly. Your decorations are an extension of who you are. Be completely authentic, and don't be afraid of being creative.

Make your room reflect all the good things about yourself and the things you like. Whether that means smothering your walls with posters or with photos, create an area to excel in. This is your space for the next ten months, so make it reflect everything *you* love.

With all that in mind, here are a couple ideas of how *not* to decorate your room:

- **The "I'm homesick" dorm room:** So, you miss your parents… most people do. Having one or two (maybe three) pictures of mom and dad is okay; having life size pictures of them plastered on every wall is not.

- **The "Barbie threw up" dorm room:** You like the color pink, a lot. In fact, you're purposefully dating a guy named Ken. But don't let the other colors in the spectrum be lonely. Try using two colors as your foundation, rather than one.

- **The "I party too much and may fail out" dorm room:** This is the room that has beer cans stacked in a pyramid and pizza boxes functioning as tables. Flashing beer sign? Yeah, stick to things can't be found on the wall of a bar.

- **The "only place to sit is my bed" dorm room:** This dorm room is just awkward. If size allows, try to have one or two other places where guests can sit when they visit (makes for cleaner sheets).

DEPRESSION

What's the difference between having a bad day and being depressed? To put it simply, a bad day is over in a day, or maybe two. But depression lasts longer and feels worse. It's when you feel sad, disinterested, and have a hard time carrying out your normal day to day activities for an extended amount of time. The opposite of depression isn't happiness; it's participation.

> **THE OPPOSITE OF DEPRESSION ISN'T HAPPINESS; IT'S PARTICIPATION.**

If you're having a bad day, things like prayer, friends, music, a good meal, exercise, or just sleep can really help. Sometimes talking with a priest or someone else you can go to for advice is very helpful.

With depression though, you can't just "snap out of it." You may need more than just a good night's sleep. People who struggle with depression often need the help of their doctor, psychologist, or medication to overcome this illness. If your body is sick and you need a doctor's help, you don't feel ashamed. The same is true when you're not feeling well in your emotions; you don't have to be embarrassed to go to a doctor about it. Call or go to your campus health center to see what services they offer.

Sometimes people experience depression and they don't know why. Other people struggle with depression because of something that happened. Both situations are tough and it can seem like things will never be better, like you'll never be happy again and life isn't worth living.

The truth is that "with God all things are possible." He created you for a purpose and you are meant to be here. Whatever you're going through, look to Christ on the cross. He went through it all. He was rejected, humiliated, abandoned, tortured, and suffered emotionally. God knows what you're going through and He understands. Cling to

Him in prayer through this tough time and He will help you through it, and send people to help you through it as well.

For those of you who may be struggling with a severe case of depression or suicidal thoughts, or know someone who is, please get help. Talk to someone about it. You can't do this alone, and there are people who want you to get better. There are usually free clinics for students that offer counseling and, if needed, can refer you to someone who will help you through this. Don't be ashamed of asking for help; there are plenty of people who struggle with depression or psychological disorders who, with help, are able to live life to the fullest.

Don't ever lose hope. You know what comes after the Crucifixion? The joy of the Resurrection.

DISCIPLINE

ATTENTION! About face! Forward march! Left, left, left, right, left...

When it comes to the word "discipline," most people tend to picture the above commands, or some other image of the military. It's tough. It's monotonous. It's boring. But, if you want to dramatically improve your life, you'll need to be disciplined. It's what makes good athletes great. It's what makes talented musicians legendary, and it's what can lead devout Christians to sainthood. Here are a few keys to being a more disciplined person:

Discipline Starts the Night Before

Do you want to be successful tomorrow? Start the process the night before. Review the next day's schedule, write down a list of things you want to accomplish, and set your alarm clock to get up at a decent hour. This will not only give you motivation to get out of bed, but it will take all the guesswork out when you're still wiping away eye boogers and can't think straight. (Quick Tip: Schedule an early morning class.)

Write It Down

Do you have places you need to be? Do you have goals you want to achieve? Do you want to ensure the best way to accomplish these things? Write them down. Get a schedule and outline the important times you need to be somewhere each day (classes, job, Mass, etc.). Put your goals in a notebook and make sure they are easily accessible. It's one thing when you say you want to do something, but it goes to a whole other level when you've written it down and it's staring you in the face. (Quick Tip: If you do this electronically, be sure to back it up.)

Follow Through

Discipline is a choice. You can say you're going to do something all you want, but if you don't follow through, you don't get anywhere. Imagine if a golfer stopped his swing right as the club was making contact with the ball. The ball wouldn't go too far. The same is true in life. If you don't follow through, you don't move forward.

DISCIPLINE IS A CHOICE.

Treat It Like a Game

Becoming a more disciplined person may not be easy, but that doesn't mean it can't be fun. It's like a competition with yourself. Be sure to have fun with it, and reward yourself when you do well. After all, you could be on the path to sainthood.

DISCIPLESHIP

Many Christians interchange the word "disciple" and "apostle," but their meanings are distinctly different. *Disciple* means "one who sits at the feet of" a teacher. A disciple is a perpetual student, constantly availing himself of the wisdom available to him through those who are more learned.

Apostle on the other hand, means "one who is sent." It's a commissioning and empowerment of a disciple to go forth, in the Teacher's name, sharing knowledge and instruction.

All of the Apostles were disciples, but not all of the disciples were called to be apostles.

That distinction is really important, still today.

You might know far more about God than anyone else on your floor or in your dorm. You might be that youth group kid who knew all the right answers, shared in every small group, and was involved in every skit. You might have gone to a Catholic high school and retained every obscure detail (Catholic or not) regarding dogma and doctrine. Don't make the mistake, however, of thinking that "knowing more than the rest" means you've somehow graduated from discipleship. You can't name yourself an apostle of the Lord. Even if you are called into leadership, apostles and disciples are not on opposing dodge ball teams. The best apostles are the ones who never forget or abandon their discipleship.

> **THE BEST APOSTLES ARE THE ONES WHO NEVER FORGET OR ABANDON THEIR DISCIPLESHIP.**

Who will you sit at the feet of? Who will you allow to continue to guide, direct, and form you as a disciple? Every disciple needs a mentor. Every apprentice needs a master (even Jedi). If you want to lead, you must continue to follow.

So how does modern discipleship "work," especially on a college campus where there might be a true lack of Catholic community or access to spiritual direction?

First, be aware of false teachers. Just because someone "knows" stuff about God doesn't mean they are following Him. Be careful whom you listen to…even some souls who teach Theology abandon personal prayer over time. Don't assume that knowledge about God equals a heart after His. Seek out people faithful to Catholic teaching who challenge you to grow in prayer as much as in knowledge.

Second, reach out to a true Spiritual Director. If there isn't a priest or religious on campus who can guide you, seek one back home. Asking for spiritual direction – even over the phone or through Skype – may not be as ideal as face to face, but it is better than nothing at all. Empower an older, wiser soul with the opportunity to walk with you and guide you to deeper levels of faithfulness.

Third, continue to learn from beyond your campus surroundings. There are dozens of well-respected, talented, orthodox Catholic priests/religious and laypeople offering substantial opportunities for online formation. Read (and share) blogs. Download podcasts and videos. Pick at least one book for spiritual reading that you actually read along with the class readings you're supposed to do. You need to be filled, but water sources exist well beyond campus.

Lastly, identify the prayer forms and experiences you're least excited about. Don't like daily Mass? Rearrange your schedule and get there a couple times a week. The rosary is not for you, you say? Pray it on the way to class a couple times a week. Don't like the Liturgy of the Hours? Download it on your phone and get after it. Confused by Scripture? Start reading the daily Gospel and pick up a book to help you understand it.

A TRUE DISCIPLE SEEKS INSTRUCTION.

A true disciple seeks instruction. Most people who are mature in the faith – as busy as they are – welcome hungry young souls seeking direction, but you have to be willing to ask.

DISCERNMENT

"What should I do?" This question is bound to come up often in your life and especially in your college years as you are becoming an adult and are faced with more decisions.

YOU SHOULD DISCERN IMPORTANT THINGS IN YOUR LIFE.

Discernment means to weigh a decision and all of the factors involved of each choice in the light of prayer and God's will for your life. You should discern important things in your life, such as your major, whether you should date someone, or your future vocation. What you'll wear in the morning or the type of cereal you'll eat isn't something to discern.

Ultimately, the decisions that are worth discerning are the ones that will have a major impact in your life. Broken up, the word "discernment" means, "to separate apart." That's what you do when you discern, you separate the pros and cons of two options in order to see which is better for you.

Discernment is tricky. It takes practice. It starts with simply asking a question. Here are some tips to help:

1. **Sit and pray about it.** Ask God what He wants for you and discipline yourself to be silent and listen.

2. **Be honest with yourself.** Don't make excuses or try to rationalize why you should do something if you know it's not what's best or healthy.

3. **Write** down the pros and cons of the situation.

4. **Be Aware.** Try to be in tune to your emotions. Do you feel peaceful? Anxious? Worried? Keep in mind that when you are in God's will, there will be supernatural peace.

5. **Use your head.** The Catholic Church encourages us to have a healthy balance of faith and *reason* in our lives. Do what makes sense for you and your situation.

6. **Talk to people whom you trust and who are older and wiser.** It helps to talk with someone who knows you well.

7. **Make a choice!** Don't use discernment as an excuse to procrastinate. God will make it evident to you if you made the wrong choice and He will lead you in a different direction. You can only discern the next step and He may have wanted you there for a period of time. If this is the case, it's time to come up with a new question to discern and start the process again!

Don't give up on discernment. Just because you don't hear the voice of God doesn't mean He isn't going to speak to you in others ways. If you practice discerning the little choices in your life, you'll be more prepared when the bigger ones come around!

DIVERSITY

The larger the campus you plan on attending, the more diverse the population. Maybe you're ready for something new and exciting. Diversity sounds like an adventure for you. Maybe you're scared out of your brain because your High School of less than 500 people has become a comfort zone for you. Regardless, here are some tips on encountering diversity in college:

Be Open: Realize that people come from different backgrounds and their way of thinking is greatly affected by the culture they grew up in. Be open to learning why different faiths or cultures believe what they do. It's easy to judge people when you don't know where they're coming from. Get to know them! *(NOTE: You don't have to compromise your morals in order to be open.)*

Challenges Are Good: When people question or challenge your opinion, your faith, or your way of thinking, take it as an opportunity to grow. Sometimes we become too comfortable in our way of life. Challenges and questions force you to remember (or look into) why you believe the things you do and act the way you act. Let diverse opinions encourage you out of a routine way of thinking and into who you truly desire to be.

Be Proactive: College is your chance to learn about different ways of life. Use your general education requirements to take a class that peaks your interest *and* helps you learn about different cultures and faiths. Don't be afraid to talk to that person next to you in class who looks and sounds different. Often times, this will lead to great discussion and potentially a lasting friendship.

> COLLEGE IS YOUR CHANCE TO LEARN ABOUT DIFFERENT WAYS OF LIFE.

Don't Be Afraid: Diversity is nothing to be afraid of. Most of us go into college with a certain way of life already set in place. As long as you are open and willing to grow, you will be okay— even in the midst of all the different people you will meet.

Most importantly, be firmly set in your Catholic beliefs, but always approach new ideas about faith with a loving heart. You don't have to agree with every person you meet, but you should try to understand where they are coming from. God created us diverse and uniquely in His image (Genesis 1:27). As we discover the individuality of each (different) person around us, we discover God. Don't let this opportunity pass you by!

DORMS

You have a 9:00 AM class Friday morning so you get up at 8:30 AM, hoping to squeeze in a shower. You live in a dorm with a communal shower, so you have to walk down the hall with your towel, clothes, and shampoo. When you get to the shower room you see it: all the carnage from Thursday night – the puke, the clogged sinks, the toilet paper in the showers, and maybe a little urine on the ground. Oh, and there's still one of the perpetrators asleep in a stall on the ground. Not every dorm will be the extreme party house, but they are not places of innocence either. Dorms are a shock experience. There are ups and downs. You share a building with a few hundred college students, it gets messy. Thankfully, God is in the mess, and He challenges us through it all.

Dorms can help you grow in many ways with some new obstacles, a little stress, and some laugh-out-loud moments. When you get those shock experiences, you learn and you adjust. When you have a roommate you fight with hourly, it's God's challenge for you to love them. If you're used to getting ready in a house with a small family, it's going to take time to adjust to living with a much larger group of people.

DORM LIFE WILL STRETCH YOU LIKE NEVER BEFORE.

Waking up and showering in a communal bathroom might be something new for you. Whatever you are used to, dorm life will stretch you like never before, especially in how you interact and deal with the people you live with. This can definitely be a blessing as you learn about all their differences.

There are some proactive things you can do to help navigate these new obstacles:

- For conflict with people in your dorms, the best solution is always praying before you speak. Approach conflicts with love and make sure that the person knows you aren't trying to belittle their side of the argument.

- Make sure both you and your dorm mate understand each other's boundaries and what's acceptable while you share the room. Knowing the expectations can avoid a lot of drama.

- Finally, make sure you know your R.A. and he/she knows you. Other than your roommate, this is the person who can most affect your dorm experience.

When you jump into this new experience it becomes even more important you don't compromise what you believe. It's easy to slip into negative peer pressure within the "dorm culture." This is where your faith – and how you live it out – will be tested the most. God wants you to love the people you live with, but that doesn't mean you do what they do. Keep your faith and allow God to stretch you in the ways He wants. It's going to be a crazy ride.

DRAMA

Did you think you left drama behind in high school? Ha! Wouldn't that be nice?

When you get involved in drama, here are a couple things to think about:

Is there a communication problem? Sometimes drama results when people don't understand each other, a situation, or a circumstance. Talk to the person you have a problem with, or who has a problem with you. Confrontation can be scary, but it's worth getting everything out in the open so that more drama won't be created.

When you need to approach someone about a conflict, try to put yourself in their shoes and understand where they're coming from. Talk about how you've been affected by this conflict and what your feelings are about it. It's helpful to approach the topic by using an "I feel... when... because... " statement so that the other person doesn't feel attacked.

Gossip is also a huge contributor to drama. Remember, if someone gossips to you they probably also gossip about you. Don't talk about people and problems that don't involve you or the person you are talking to. It tears apart friendships and ruins the reputations of others.

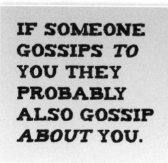

IF SOMEONE GOSSIPS *TO* YOU THEY PROBABLY ALSO GOSSIP *ABOUT* YOU.

Are your friends helping you to be a better person? If the majority of people you hang out with don't have the same values as you, you'll probably have more drama in your life simply because of these differences. That does not mean you should never reach out to other people. What it does mean is that those people you spend a lot of your time with will help determine what kind of person you become and what you have to deal with on a day-to-day basis.

You can't please everyone. It's a hopeless cause to try to make everyone happy all the time. Jesus didn't say it would be easy to follow Him and that everyone would like us. He said it would be hard and that we would be persecuted. When you choose to do the right thing, it can, unfortunately, come with drama because people won't agree with you. You have to have a tough skin to be a Catholic on your campus. If you're doing the right thing, try to not let the drama bother you.

DRUGS

What is often unseen in college is the reality that the decisions you are making and the freedom you are exercising demand a response that reflects your character, faith, and morals.

It may never come to a point where you are standing before someone who is offering you drugs or other illegal substances. You may be taking time to read this because you *have* experienced that moment. Whatever the case may be, the truth is that your daily decisions are either going to lead you to or away from situations like this one. Truth be told, no matter where you go there will more than likely be a group of people abusing substances, but there will also be people calling you on to better things.

If you are struggling, there is Good News! Our Catholic faith is rich with forgiveness and mercy. God the Father desires for your reconciliation with His Son. If you fall in this struggle, run to the cross. That is where Christ meets our sins and conquers them.

With any struggle, God always provides a way to freedom. With any temptation, it is good for us to stop and take time to be honest with ourselves, in light of the Truth the Church gives us, and examine our lives. Maybe you can take time each week to answer the question: Am I moving closer to Christ through these decisions or away from Him?

Make sure you take time to be honest with your close friends, or people you are in close relationship with, and they can get you help. Typically, someone who is not currently struggling with the same or a similar addiction is best. It is not that they are superior to those who are struggling with something in particular, but we each struggle with different things and their lack of struggle gives them strength to be

YOU ARE NOT ALONE.

a good foothold of truth in your life. Attempt to avoid occasions of sin; that is to say, if you know you struggle when in specific situations, work hard to avoid putting yourself in those situations. Surround yourself with peers and mentors who point you to the Lord and His plan for you.

Galatians 5:1 says, "For freedom, Christ set us free; so stand firm and do not submit again to the yoke of slavery." Know above all that you are not alone and that God has a plan in store for your salvation. Commit to the victory that has already been won for you, and you will see the fruit of the Lord's vindication (labor) in your life.

FAITH

Your faith in college will be put to the test. No one will kick you out of school if you decide to stop practicing your faith. Mom and Dad are not there to make sure that you are going to Mass, nor is anyone else. The decision to be a faithful, active Catholic college student is completely up to you.

Many of your professors and classmates will have perspectives that differ from the Catholic faith, and they will try to convince you of their "truth." Now is the time to solidify what you believe, learn about your faith, and deepen it.

You need to be honest with yourself: where is your faith today? Where do you need to grow? To help you, here are three aspects that are essential to maintaining a strong faith while in college:

Prayer:
Prayer is not simply saying words you have memorized when life is miserable. Prayer is a relationship with a person – with the God who is madly in love with you. If you have never prayed before or don't know how to pray, start somewhere. Set aside five or ten minutes of your day, and ask the Lord to reveal Himself to you. Perhaps read and reflect on the readings for daily Mass. To put it simply, do something!

Mass:
Going to Mass every Sunday is essential. The Church tells us that the Eucharist is the source and summit of our Catholic faith, the highest and most perfect prayer. Some schools have chapels where daily Mass is celebrated on certain days of the week; others have Mass times that are geared toward students. Take advantage of these opportunities to deepen your relationship with Christ.

If Mass isn't offered on your campus, find a Catholic church nearby and look up their Mass schedule. Make it a priority to go, even if it's a little out of your way.

HE IS NOT A WAY AMONG VARIOUS OTHER WAYS... HE IS *THE* WAY, *THE* TRUTH, AND *THE* LIFE.

Reconciliation:

Sin is sadly a part of our life as human beings. None of us are as holy or as virtuous as we ought to be. The Sacrament of Reconciliation allows us to receive the forgiveness and mercy of Christ. It is gives us strength to avoid sin and to conquer temptations. Therefore, going to Reconciliation monthly is a great way to stay faithful and stay in the state of grace.

Jesus Christ does not present Himself as a truth among truths, or a way among various other ways. He states that He is the way, the truth, and the life (John 14:6). Seek Him, call upon Him, follow Him, and place your faith in Him.

FAILURE

"Failure is not an option!"— Infamous words from a competitive father who apparently didn't understand that the cutthroat game of UNO with his seven-year-old might not be the best opportunity to share such wisdom. Talk about pressure to succeed.

You might feel the same confusion and heightened level of stress during your academic years as a college student. There will be sections within your major that won't make very much sense, they'll be tough as nails, and you might get poor grades at times. But due to your obedience to authority you'll keep pushing through, right? Get real.

Failing stinks, especially if you're used to succeeding. Our Lord wants us to be joyful, not pitiful. Failure is hard to face head-on, but it shouldn't steal your joy. Rather, it should come with an eagerness to take a deep breath, pick yourself up, and try again. Once you've mentally acknowledged you've failed, say this out loud:

"I failed."

Once you admit to something, you can get over it and move forward. Trust me, everyone fails at some point. The enemy wants you to dwell on your shortcomings and lull around in a pity party. Seriously, you're no dummy, but because this is so simple you're going to fight it and add words in there, like:

ONCE YOU ADMIT TO SOMETHING, YOU CAN GET OVER IT AND MOVE FORWARD.

"I'm stupid and failed."

"My hair smells like tacos and I failed."

"Nobody likes me because I failed."

"Even auto correct on my phone said I failed so I must be a failed."

Here are some great ways to overcome failing:

- Communicate with your professors or TA's, especially if you are struggling to understand the material..

- Be sure you're asking questions.

- Learn to take good notes in class.

- Find a study group. Odds are that others are struggling too.

- Ask for intersession from St. Aloysius Gonzaga (patron of Catholic youth), St. Jerome (patron of students), or St. Ambrose (patron of learning).

- Access the Sacraments often (Reconciliation, Eucharist).

- Seek counsel. Don't emotionally isolate yourself.

Life is full of lessons you'll either pick up right away or that will knock you down. Always remember to take a deep breath, pick yourself up, and try again, because "Failure is not an option!"

FINANCES

At this stage of your life, you should have had some sort of education on how to manage your money. The adolescent days of blowing your money on baseball cards and lip-gloss should have run their course. Mature spending and saving are in full effect, right? Psssfff, as if.

Learning to manage what little finances you have now will make life a lot easier after you finish college. Conforming to the "provident" approach to spending during your college life will be the best decision you'll ever make.

Provident Spending 101:

1. **Make a budget and stick to it.** There are zillions of free budgeting tools for college students online. Organizations employed by financially savvy people are out there to help guide young, college-aged people through the awkwardness of money management.

2. **Shop with a purpose.** Coupons rock! Generic is the brand of choice. This will help you avoid compulsive spending.

3. **Do everything you can to pay with cash.** Credit cards can be deceiving. You can establish credit other ways than with a high-interest piece of plastic. If you do have a credit card, be smart, use it sparingly, and pay off the balance each month.

4. **Surround yourself with financially like-minded people.** Regularly hanging out with financially unstable people is tempting because they make spending money irresponsibly seem so fun.

FINANCIAL MODESTY IS ATTRACTIVE AND SHOULD BE HELD IN HIGH REGARD.

5. **Observe** the spending habits of the opposite sex, especially those

of people you might want to date. Financial modesty is attractive and should be held in high regard.

6. **Don't lend money to friends and expect to see it again.** At first, the behavior resembles borrowing, and then it slowly develops into taking all they can get. Just be cautious.

7. **Beware of the temptation to over-borrow on student loans.** It may seem like a great idea to increase the borrowed amount by a couple thousand dollars each semester to get some new clothes or a TV. Remember, you will have to pay that back, with interest, at some point.

There is no shame in being wise with your money. There will always be naysayers who will try to discourage you along the way, so stay strong. Surprisingly, money is mentioned in the Bible more than 800 times. Crack that puppy open and rest in the added security that God has your back too.

FITNESS

You'll never see a koala on the logo of a gym, not even in Australia. The fact that koalas average about twenty hours of sleep a day makes them less than ideal as a fitness mascot. A couple of months into college you might feel as though you're part koala, finding your oh-so-comfortable mattress an alluring alternative to that biology lab.

Even some who were true "athletes" in high school stop working out in college if not actively involved with varsity or club sports.

It's always easier *not* to work out. There's always "something else" to do. And koalas are cute, after all…so what's the big deal, really?

In fact, if our bodies really are "temples of the Holy Spirit" as St. Paul attests (1 Corinthians 6:19), then the bigger the temple, the more glory we give to God, right?

Um…no, not exactly. Fitness is about far more than weight or laziness.

Fitness is about health of mind, body, and soul. Your body is a temple, and whether a tiny chapel or a glorious cathedral, it's meant to be a worthy dwelling place for Christ (specifically in the Eucharist), healthy and balanced. In honoring our body (the gift) we honor our God (the Giver).

> **FITNESS IS ABOUT HEALTH OF MIND, BODY, AND SOUL.**

Now, rest is good, yes. Rest is commanded, in fact (See Exodus 20:8, 11). That being said, much of our fatigue is not a result of a healthy lifestyle but an unhealthy one (which we deal with more in the entry on Food – page 83).

The more active you stay, the healthier you are going to be and feel. That doesn't mean overextending yourself or getting involved in every possible activity, either (we deal with that in the entry on Time Management – page 145).

This also doesn't mean you have to live at the gym. (That much exposure to bleach, self-tanning spray, silicone, and chlorine isn't good for anyone.)

Staying active and keeping fit means keeping busy and getting your heart rate up. Go for a run. Commit to doing push-ups and sit-ups every day. Enroll in a (Pontius) Pilates class or get involved in intramural sports. Get a few people from your floor together at set times and exercise together. The more people, the more accountability you'll have. Snowing outside, you say? Get a DVD workout program and move that ten-dollar coffee table out of the way. Not athletic, you say? Find a treadmill, grab your favorite book, and take a quick-paced walk. You can even download a podcast from LifeTeen.com and grow in your faith while you work up a sweat.

Staying active and getting fit has benefits well beyond weight control, too:

- A regular workout schedule forces you to better manage your time, maintains a higher metabolism, and allows you to burn more calories even when at rest.

- Regular elevations of heart rate promote a healthier overall sleep schedule. The more often and harder you work out, the more deeply you sleep. In fact, shorter stints of deeper sleep outweigh the benefits of longer bouts of sleep (to any koalas out there).

- The release of endorphins through increased physical activity sharpens your thinking and promotes a healthier heart and immune system.

- Better overall fitness translates to greater self-confidence, security, and mental balance in your personality and daily outlook.

- Exercise offers you yet another form of prayer outside of Church each day if you invite Him into it, while also offering a tremendous witness to others of balance, healthiness, and respect for your bodily temple.

This is the only temple you get…respect and honor it. It's designed to bring God glory. Never forget, "…you were bought with a price. So glorify God in your **body**" (1 Corinthians 6:20).

FOOD

The world's first "argument" was over something to eat. Adam and Eve's appetite (for self) was their downfall. Luckily for us, God had a plan to set things straight. Christ introduced a new plan to satisfy our appetites like never before and, not surprisingly, it too involved something to "eat," so to speak. Thank God for the Eucharist.

We are corporal beings; we are souls with bodies, and those bodies have needs. Obviously without water and food we cease to exist, but there's a huge discrepancy between eating to live and living to eat.

When we eat, what we eat, and how much we eat all have tangible effects on our mood, health, energy, and general attitude.

WE ARE SOULS WITH BODIES, AND THOSE BODIES HAVE NEEDS.

Everyone's heard of "the freshman fifteen," referring to the common weight gain most new undergrads go through when moving away from home. All of a sudden, the least healthy option in the dining hall is the most popular choice. Late-night pizza deliveries and quick runs to the drive-thru do little to increase our vitamin intake or maintain a balanced diet. It's not that a little weight gain is the end of the world or that every meal has to represent every level of the food pyramid, but over time poor dietary choices begin to affect more than just the waistline.

A heightened awareness of what you are not eating (and the vitamins and nutrients you are or are not getting) might reveal a surprising amount about your mood, energy, and overall productivity.

Here are just a few quick facts regarding daily diet trends:

- Heightened intake of caffeine dehydrates you.

- A lack of water stresses and impairs your kidney function, leaving your body more toxic.

- Refined white flour (like in pizza) slows your metabolism, taxes your digestive system, and makes you more mentally sluggish.

- Soda (even diet soda) often ends up making you eat even more by shutting down your cerebral inhibitor, causing the false belief that your body is still hungry.

- The nutritious benefit of salad is severely diminished by the high fat content in most dressing.

- A lack of fresh fruits and vegetables leaves your body more acidic than alkaline, leaving you far more prone to sickness and even cancer.

- Highly processed foods (i.e. most "fast food"), foods with hydrogenated and partially hydrogenated oils, and white flours (like most bread and buns) all release free radicals into your body. Free radicals destroy cells, damage your DNA, and alter your biochemical compounds. They affect your mood, alter your hormone levels, cause fatigue, speed up the aging process, worsen some allergies, and are linked to everything from heart disease to cancer.

None of these facts mean you have to eliminate every possible unhealthy food from your life – especially considering that your campus options might be limited. What it necessitates, though, is that you are mindful about what you eat. Strive for balance. Opt for fresh fruit over Fruit Loops. Choose to dip some salad in dressing rather than drowning the greens in it. Try a wheat crust pizza or, better yet, fast from it late at night and offer it up to God. Leave mac-n-cheese in your room as the last resort and walk to a dining hall for exercise and more options.

Take note, too, of how different foods affect your mood and your energy level. Do what Adam and Eve should have and become more aware of how food (or the lack of it) has an effect on your life, both good and bad. And take advantage of the food that heaven offers you – the true Bread of Life – available only at the Lord's altar table. Never turn down that invitation to dinner.

FREEDOM

Can you imagine growing up with no bedtime? No one telling you how much dessert you can eat? When your friends have to go home? Nobody telling you that you can't be alone with your boyfriend/girlfriend in your room? Well, welcome to college. It is every middle school kid's dream come true: more freedom then your 13-year-old self ever thought possible. But the truth is that you are not 13, and "freedom" unchecked can be life altering. Even a fictional superhero (Superman) understood that "with great power comes great responsibility."

You never really stop to think about why you have a bedtime growing up, or a curfew. You never really stop to consider why your parents make you go to Mass. For most people these things feel like arbitrary restrictions on how much fun you can have. But the truth is those "arbitrary restrictions" gave you the freedom to not feel awful and exhausted through your younger years. Rules about not being alone in your room with a girlfriend/boyfriend gave you the freedom to not worry about if you were going to be a parent. And regular participation in your faith gave you a relationship with Christ that most people will only hunger for. Most of what your parents "made" you do was to give you greater freedom in the long run.

But here's the thing: the training wheels are off. You are riding solo. If you decide not to go to sleep, you have the freedom to stay up all night. Don't want to do your reading? No one will make you. Stayed out Saturday night and feel like sleeping through Mass on Sunday? Your call. Want to sleep over at a "friend's" room? You can…but don't think it is without cost.

The reality is that true freedom is not doing whatever you want, but having

> **TRUE FREEDOM IS NOT DOING WHATEVER YOU WANT, BUT HAVING THE OPPORTUNITY TO DO WHAT IS TRULY BEST FOR YOU.**

the opportunity to do what is truly best for you. Sure, you can choose not to do your reading, but you will more than likely fail the class, and then you will lose the freedom to move on to the next level. Stop going to Mass and you will become disconnected from your faith and your relationship with Christ will slowly fade. Yes, you can sleep around, but you might lose your freedom from having an STD, or your freedom to choose when you want to be a parent. Get the picture? "Freedom"(in the eyes of the world) can cost you the true Freedom (that Christ gives).

So, exercise your freedom wisely. It sounds crazy, but give yourself a curfew. Make rules for yourself about who can be in the room alone with you. Schedule when you are going to get your work done. You have the freedom to be whoever you want to be. Decide who that is, and use your freedom to get there.

FRIENDS

Distance doesn't destroy friendships, but it definitely makes them harder; and when you pile on a bunch of new people you just met, it becomes even more difficult to maintain your old friendships. If you start to get frustrated with trying to balance the old with the new don't worry, it's normal. Unless everyone from your high school goes to the same college as you then you're going to fall out of touch with people. You might feel guilty about making new friends or spending time with them when you could video chat with the old ones, but this is a moment of trust. You have to trust that your friends really are your friends and you have to trust God that He is bringing the right people into your life. God gives us the exact amount of time that we need to spend with each person in our lives.

It's a given that you're going to have to dive in and make new friends. You have to grow in the new setting. That definitely doesn't mean dropping the friends you've already made, but staying in touch shouldn't stress you out. Remember, God is in control and He wants to bring you into the best friendships possible. He is not trying to take anything away from you, just give you something better.

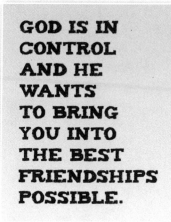

GOD IS IN CONTROL AND HE WANTS TO BRING YOU INTO THE BEST FRIENDSHIPS POSSIBLE.

This is a time to honor your old friends while making new ones. It's definitely a challenge, but an exciting one. Rest easy knowing God's got the wheel.

Some practical tips on the actual friend making:

1. **Say yes!** Go to all the university-sanctioned "welcome-week" events that you can. A lot of them will be very, very lame and extremely awkward, but everyone will go to them, and if you say no you'll miss out on meeting the most people you can.

2. **Keep your door open.** Maybe make a sign that says come in and say hi. Appear friendly and eager to your neighbors around you. Everyone is just as lonely as you are, and if you make even the tiniest effort, you'll be surprised how many people stop by. Also, make an effort to stop into other people's room—they won't always come to you. Take the initiative and meet people!

3. **Get numbers.** Get at least one person's number in each of your first classes. You can be nonchalant and say you want to exchange numbers in case either of you misses class or has a question. Trust me, no one will say no to this. Then you can easily text them and you have a study buddy for the rest of the semester, which can easily blossom into an awesome friendship.

4. **Go to Mass a few times a week.** Lift up all the people you've met over the previous days. Hang around by the chapel after Mass and introduce yourself to the other Catholic students. Find out when the Newman events or Catholic club meetings are and show up! These will be the friends who can help you grow in your faith.

5. **Reach out.** Lastly, if you notice someone not adjusting well in your dorm (or wherever), invite them along with you. Reach out to the lonely. It's a fun place to be and you could really make a difference in their lives. Sometimes all someone needs is an invitation.

FUN

Fun is an interesting word. Secular society likes to twist it and mess with what it really means. The world makes it easy to think something is fun when it actually is something harmful. There's a trap of having the wrong kind of fun and becoming more miserable than before. This happens in college especially, when people tell you how this is the time you can let loose and no one will hold it against you. College is the time for reckless, juvenile, and sinful fun, right? Some people have that "sin now, repent later" mentality going into college, all for the sake of fun. This is dangerous because it's a lie to yourself.

Don't call something fun to cover up how negative it is. If it's a sin then you know it's bad; calling it "fun" doesn't make it okay. God wants you to have fun in a holy, loving, and fulfilling way that gives you lasting happiness. This is what will help you live out your college career successfully.

Fun (*noun*): Enjoyment, amusement, or lighthearted pleasure.

God wants everything in this definition for you and more! He wants this fun to last, to lead you to sainthood, and for it not to become a regretted memory. Does such fun exist? Surely, it does!

Here are a few tips for how holy fun works: first, it should be legal, which means no drugs, underage drinking, or other law breaking. Second, you should be able to remember it, so I repeat, no alcohol. If you wake up the next day with a hangover and chunks of your night forgotten then it wasn't the fun God wants. Third, the people you spend time with should be seeking holy fun just like you. This helps a lot when you have friends that have the same goal you have.

Following these tips will help avoid a lot of the wrong kind of fun so you can seek out the right kind. Do you want to be a part of the clubbing party scene or will you have holy fun with good people? There are so many better ways to enjoy your time in college than the typical ways that might run through your mind.

Go to a concert of your favorite musicians. You can also enjoy more college sports games. If your college doesn't have a big athletic push, then there's still fun in the local community. There are festivals, coffee houses, and other great ways to have fun. There is even the option of swing dancing. Some guys might be against this but in large groups swing dancing can be a great way to have fun.

GOD WANTS YOU TO HAVE FULFILLING FUN.

Seek out God in how you have fun and your college experience will be so much more than what you expect it to be. God wants you to have fulfilling fun.

GREEK LIFE

Alpha, Beta, Gamma, huh?

Yes, we're talking about Greek life, not the
radiation waves of your high school physics
class. But some of the things surrounding
fraternities and sororities may seem, well, like
Greek.

**ALPHA,
BETA,
GAMMA,
HUH?**

Who are the Greeks?
Even though they're not from Greece, you may
find a toga or two. The "Greeks" are the college
men and women on your campus who joined a
fraternity or sorority. You'll find Greeks in every major and many other
campus organizations.

What do fraternities and sororities do?
College will open up a whole new set of pressures to do what
everyone else is doing. Greek life can compound all of these pressures,
especially to drink and to "hook up," simply by exposing you more
to it more. There's no denying it, fraternities and sororities are social
organizations. They have mixers, date parties, formals, and other
organized social events.

But there's more to it than that. Greeks are involved in many activities
on campus and in the community, such as homecoming and
other school-sponsored events. All have philanthropic or service
opportunities, which raise money to support local or national charities,
or give back to the community. Each Greek organization has leadership
opportunities, as well as brotherhood and sisterhood events to build
community.

How does this affect my faith?
College and Greek life will give you a chance to meet many new
people, people who will challenge your thinking about life and faith
and people who will bring new ideas and ways to do things. This can

provide an opportunity to fully explore and to grow deeper in your faith.

You'll have an opportunity to evangelize and reach out to the same people who challenge you. Living your life as a holy, Catholic college student is enough to make any person turn their head and ask questions.

Fraternities and sororities can be a new support system for you. Building faith relationships and friendships is key to a holy life. Sisters and brothers can go with you to Mass, Adoration, and Reconciliation. They can be people who join you for Bible studies or praise and worship nights. If your organization doesn't have a faith group—start one.

How do I know if it is for me?
First pray about it and think about it. Only you can make the decision. Greek life isn't for everyone. The most important thing is to surround yourself with people who love and support you. If you decide to join a Greek organization, join one where you feel most comfortable being who God made you to be.

HOMESICKNESS

For many people, going to college may be the first time they've been away from their family and friends for extended periods of time. Leaving your home, your family, your friends, and even your bed can create a sense of loss, or homesickness. This is normal! You've been surrounded by the same people, places, and routines for the past 18 years. Naturally, you're going to feel strange about not having these things anymore.

HOMESICKNESS CAN TAKE DIFFERENT FORMS.

Homesickness can take different forms – not being able to sleep, not being able to eat, not wanting to talk to your friends, crying uncontrollably, or even feeling depressed. However, this doesn't mean you have to sit in your dorm room and stare at a picture of the two cats you left at home.

One of the best things you can do as a new student on campus is to get involved. Be prudent and avoid throwing yourself into every club you can just to try and forget about home. Instead, take some time to talk to current members of the organizations and discuss the purpose of the club and the time commitment. Pick a few things you think you might like and try them out. If you don't like a certain group, you can always remove yourself from it and try something else until you find one that you enjoy.

Another important thing to remember is that professors and university employees are there to help you. There's nothing wrong with calling Mom and Dad or a high school friend, but there may be people who can offer you more help when you can't find a building, lose your dorm key, or miss a test. Rather than feeling like you're never going to get the hang of things, learn to ask for help and you'll be surprised at how much you can learn from others.

One significant building that can make any new place feel like home is the Church. It may look different, smell different, and be filled with different people, but Jesus is the same no matter where you are. You can find surprising comfort in the familiarity of the Mass. Not to mention it's a great place to meet college-aged students who love the Lord!

Before you know it, you're going to make lots of new friends, go many new places, and learn new things about yourself. College is a place to build on the foundation our parents gave us at home to discover the person God created us to be.

HYGIENE

Most people – even those who don't read Scripture – have heard of Job. Few people in the Bible had a worse time than Job did; his life makes even the saddest country songs sound like a nursery rhyme.

One fact that only those who read the Bible know, however, is that in addition to Job's calamitous life, he also had bad breath.

"My breath is abhorred by my wife…" (Job 19:17)

As if losing his family, home, wealth, and health wasn't bad enough, the brother apparently had some wicked halitosis, too. Luckily for Job, God's mercy was bigger than even that.

Only four out of five dentists might agree on a particular toothpaste, but five out of five agree that brushing is necessary, for many reasons.

If surveyed, five out of five roommates and classmates would likewise say that showers are not only encouraged, but also necessary.

Regardless of whether the "messy" look is in or if your roommate does not comprehend the concept of saving some hot water, personal hygiene is a non-negotiable in college. Your family is morally obligated to love you; those in your dorm or apartment complex are not.

Making time to cleanse and groom yourself does more than keep those around you from having to invest in gas masks or hazmat suits, too; good personal hygiene demonstrates an unending respect for yourself, not just others.

God's command to "love your neighbor as yourself" could easily be

> **GOD'S COMMAND TO "LOVE YOUR NEIGHBOR AS YOURSELF" COULD EASILY BE APPLIED TO PERSONAL HEALTH AND CARE.**

applied to personal health and care, as well. It's one thing to miss a shower one morning because the snooze button won the war of wills. It's quite another to repeatedly miss that morning shower out of sheer laziness, thereby forcing those within a six foot radius to wage their own war against distraction whilst trying to take notes during class.

Taking care of yourself insures that others don't have to have "the conversation" with you, straining an already fragile living situation to its unnecessary limits.

That being said, if you're the clean one and your roommate, suitemate, or floor mate is the one who is olfactorily challenged, proceed with caution and with mercy. You never know, they might have actually been raised on a farm, so take that into consideration before you make any unnecessary allusions to pig pens or manure trucks.

Saying, "Hey, do you want to wash your sheets and towels when I do?" sounds a lot less offensive than, "Are you hosting a biology experiment under your comforter?"

Offering, "If you want to shower first so you have enough hot water" is a lot less demeaning than, "Tell you what, you sit on the couch with this bar of soap and I'll just turn on the fire hose."

Throwing out, "Will you tell me when my hair gets a little out of control, I don't want to force anyone else to deal with it" is a lot more charitable and exemplary than saying, "At the rate you're going, small birds will be nesting in there in no time. That 'do' is a don't."

You get the idea.

It's important to be comfortable with yourself, absolutely, just not at the expense of those you've been called to share space with. Respect others by respecting yourself.

IDENTITY

College is innately a time of growth. It's a new environment. Everything changes. There is a newfound freedom that comes from living on your own, away from your family, the place you grew up in, and all familiarity.

However, there is something that is unchanging in the midst of all the change. Your identity stays the same, regardless of your age, state in life, or what situation you are in. You are, and will always be, a beloved son or daughter of a heavenly King. Your identity never changes, and everything flows from that reality.

> YOU ARE, AND WILL ALWAYS BE, A BELOVED SON OR DAUGHTER OF A HEAVENLY KING.

As people get to know you, questions will come up about who you are, where you're from, and what you like and don't like. Or maybe these same questions will arise just as your mind naturally responds to all the external change. Establishing yourself as a young adult in this world, whether you know it or not, is exactly what you're doing when you answer questions like these.

There are a lot of realizations that come with growing up and leaving everything behind. You realize your true strengths, as all the walls and comfort zones you've built throughout the years come tumbling down. You realize exactly what you're bad at as you try out new things that you may have never done before like laundry, or setting a diet for yourself, or doing homework without anyone checking up on you.

Regardless of where you grew up, or which high school you went to, God has created you uniquely and with a specific purpose. Your strengths and weaknesses were thought out when God made you. Seek Him and you will become more fully who God created you to be; you will, as Blessed John Paul II said, "become who you are."

Whatever the reason, however the questions about whom you are come up, turn to Our Lord. It would be such a shame for you to not let Him into this exciting time of your life. For the first time in a long time, by virtue of your college freedom, you can be totally and completely open to whom He wants you to be. He wants to change you; listen to Him and He will guide you. My brothers and sisters, hold fast to Christ with all that you are. Never forget Whose you are, and no matter how vast or subtle the change or understanding of your identity comes, it will be good because it is rooted in Him who gives nothing but truth and everlasting life.

INTEGRITY

One of the greatest things about college is that many things are different than high school. Unfortunately these differences can often lead to the temptation to dismiss all your values and everything you've learned in order to "find yourself" and become a "completely new person."

Make no mistake about it: you will be tested while you're in college. Your faith, your morals, and your integrity will be challenged in a variety of ways, even if you're at a Christian or Catholic school. So if you want to be a person of integrity, there are several things that you need to remember:

Integrity Requires Consistency

Have you ever met someone who said one thing and did the exact opposite? It probably drove you crazy. Having integrity means that your actions and your words match up in ALL situations. You must be consistent whether you're at Mass, at work, in class, or hanging out with friends on a Friday night. And, by the way, this includes your Facebook and Twitter accounts.

> **HAVING INTEGRITY MEANS THAT YOUR ACTIONS AND YOUR WORDS MATCH UP IN ALL SITUATIONS.**

We're All Hypocrites

With that said, it's also important to note that you won't find one person who isn't hypocritical. Now this doesn't give you an excuse to go out and do whatever you want, but, ultimately, you will make mistakes. The bad news is that you won't ever be able to have perfect integrity. The good news is that God gives you tools to improve, which is why He created the Sacrament of Reconciliation.

Seek the Sacrament of Reconciliation Regularly

If there's one thing that can lead you toward greater integrity, it's the Sacrament of Reconciliation. Think about it. The Savior of the world is waiting to forgive all your sins if you simply come before Him. So find your school's Newman Center or a local Catholic parish and write down the times they offer the Sacrament of Reconciliation. There's no better way to become a more consistent person than by confessing the times you've been inconsistent.

JOBS

It is such a blessing to have a refrigerator stocked with food, but when you need money in college you are faced with a choice: either call home and beg, or get a job.

Before you pick up the phone to plead with your parents to send you cash, consider the many benefits of becoming a productive member of your college workforce.

> **WHEN YOU NEED MONEY IN COLLEGE YOU ARE FACED WITH A CHOICE: EITHER CALL HOME AND BEG, OR GET A JOB.**

Study Time AND Work Time
Most college jobs will let you study for your classes when you're not busy. Yes, that means you get dedicated study time *and* you get paid for it.

Get Scheduled
Having a fixed work schedule forces you to make your own and to create a routine – and routine is good. Knowing you have to work all afternoon will make you plan the rest of your day so you still have time to study, pray, and hang out with your friends.

Positive Involvement = Positive Benefits
Having a job on campus increases the likelihood that you will meet people who share common interests with you. The shared experience of a job opens up opportunities for friendship and conversation. Not only that, having a job on campus can connect you with people who could later on write you great letters of recommendation, or can help you line up jobs after you graduate. Being able to prove that you are a good worker to the manager of your campus job now can help you reap great rewards *later*.

Money
Yes, it is nice to have money and not have to ask your parents for it. Being able to buy a cup of coffee in the union, pay for a movie, or go

on a date with that girl or guy in your chemistry class without having to call your parents to get money is freedom, and it will make your college experience far more enjoyable.

Jobs open up all the time on campus, so check your student newspaper or school website for job openings and start applying. Your bank account (and your parents) will thank you later.

LAZINESS

One of the most tempting traps that anyone can fall into is a day of doing absolutely nothing. A day without a schedule can easily turn into a day where nothing actually happens. Sometimes a day like this is needed after a week of exams or a rushed paper deadline, but this is more rare than you think. It's incredibly enticing to do nothing except have a big bowl of Lucky Charms and watch reruns of *The Office*, but does that really glorify God?

> **A DAY WITHOUT A SCHEDULE CAN EASILY TURN INTO A DAY WHERE NOTHING ACTUALLY HAPPENS.**

College isn't about making enough free time so you can be lazy for an entire weekend. You need to take advantage of every moment and make it worth something. Laziness is a trap that most students fall into, but when you're in college it's worse because don't have your old friends or family pushing you to get out of bed and go do something.

If you start to give in to doing nothing, don't be surprised when it affects the rest of your days. You can't keep up with the two extremes of doing nothing and then having a packed day of classes and homework. Eventually, the laziness will make you resent the busy days. If you resent the work you have to do, then the quality will decline. It is a battle of your will. It's a battle between you and a snooze button. It's a battle between sleeping in on your free day or going to daily Mass.

The more you give into laziness, the harder it is to regain the ambition to be productive. You need to be able to say yes or no when it matters, and with full self-control. Laziness is a test of the will and there are a few ways to make sure you're ready for that test.

When you know that you have a free day, have at least two tasks that you want to accomplish during that day. It can be simple, like taking out your trash, or it could be something more time consuming, like having an hour of exercise time. As long as you have some thing to motivate you, then you can keep your will strong.

Another thing that will help is not packing your school days with all the work. Spread out your assignments so you can have some free time on class days too.

The goal isn't to go through college by cramming and sleep binging. Laziness doesn't fit with what God wants and it won't help you be successful in the coming years.

LEARNING TO SAY "NO"

NO! Such a wonderful word. In Spanish? NO! Italian? Still NO! What about French? You guessed it: NO! There is such a simple beauty there. Two letters with such awesome power. But for many college students, the power of this word gets lost. There are just so many good things to do. So many causes to support. So many friends to hang out with. So many activities to be a part of. And those are the good things. The reality, however, is that college is also home to a number of things that should get your strong no. It can be overwhelming.

So, let's start with the obvious places for you to use the awesome power of your no. Some stuff out there is just not good for you. A yes in these situations can be disastrous. So here is a good rule: anything that could negatively affect the rest of your life (or eternity) should probably get a no. Some obvious things to say no to are: sex (unless you are married), drugs (including abusing prescription drugs), and underage or irresponsible drinking. You will notice that not everyone says no to these things. They will pay the consequence for it either with addictions they never wanted, memories they will never get rid of, and scars that go deeper than what you can see with your eyes. You don't need that. A momentary high, with a lifetime of possible consequence, is not worth it. It is a good idea to decide to say no to these things now.

But some choices are not so obvious. You will quickly become acquainted with the hundreds of credit card applications you will get in the mail and find around campus. They will promise everything from T-shirts to trips to Hawaii if you sign up. Seems like a good idea, but abusing credit can hurt your future. Might be a good place for a no.

The thing is, there are a lot of good things in college. And some of them will require you to say no as well. For instance, you have a final tomorrow and you are not ready. A bunch of kids from the Newman Center are heading out to feed the homeless. What to do? Well, considering the test is tomorrow and you are not ready, you should probably stay home and study. Learning to say no, even to good

KNOWING WHEN TO SAY NO CAN MEAN THE DIFFERENCE BETWEEN GETTING THE FUTURE YOU ARE PLANNING ON AND GETTING THE FUTURE YOU ENDED UP WITH.

things, is an important part of life. Does that mean you should never go out and do service? Absolutely not; but it might mean you have to say no to something else in order to study ahead of time so you can feed the homeless the day before a final.

Knowing when to say no can mean the difference between getting the future you are planning on and getting the future you ended up with. So, learn to use your no.

MAJOR/MINOR

It's finally time to make some important life decisions. The hottest topic of discussion for college students seems to be, "what's your major?" The first thing to know about your area of study is that there is always room for a change of mind (or heart). Ask five alumni if they changed their majors during college, and four out of five will likely say that they did.

When it comes to your major there are two types of college students: the ones who know exactly what they want and the ones who don't.

For the Ones Who Don't Know What They Want

Choose your passion. If you aren't passionate about anything, then you should probably figure that out first. Pray about it. Take a class to test your interests. Spend some time discovering your passions! It's easy to just enter the field that runs in the family or do what you feel pressured to do because you don't know where else to start. But God doesn't put desires on your heart without reason, and He has a specific purpose for you (Jeremiah 29:11).

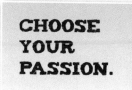

CHOOSE YOUR PASSION.

For the Ones Who Know Exactly What They Want

You're in a good place, but check your intentions. Why are you choosing/changing your major? Have you taken any time to pray about it? While God places many good desires on our hearts to lead us down His path, the world and the enemy also place misguided desires on our heart. God can make crooked lines straight (Isaiah 42:16), but it's much easier if you start on the straight line.

Changing Your Major and Adding a Minor

Don't be afraid to change your major or to add a minor. If your original plan isn't working out, changing your major may be exactly what you need to get back on track.

Adding a minor is a great way to diversify your studies and add some life to a strict schedule of major-specific courses. Look at the list of

> **DON'T BE AFRAID TO CHANGE YOUR MAJOR OR TO ADD A MINOR.**

minors offered and see if anything appeals to you.

School counselors can be a huge help with the logistics of all this, but are often not the best place to go for advice on what you should actually choose. Go to people who know you well and get several opinions on the situation. The school counselor might look at what *makes sense*, but your friends, family, and God will look at what is best for you. Once you know what's best for you, a counselor should be able to offer options to help you pursue your desires.

MEDIA CONSUMPTION

Be honest, is this you? While you do your homework you have your Internet browser open with e-mail, Facebook, and Twitter tabs open and ready to check. iTunes is playing some new music you downloaded, and in the background of all of this, the TV is on so you can make sure you don't miss you don't miss American Idol. While this is going on your phone is buzzing every few minutes with updates, notifications, and text messages from your friends.

It is time to *simplify* and take away distractions so you can focus on the most important things first. It is not about cutting all of those other things out of your life, it is prioritizing things so you can be the most effective. With all of that surrounding you, 30 minutes of homework can easily turn into two hours of distracted studying.

Here are some tips:

1. **Close down all other windows on your computer when doing homework:** Eliminate the temptation to be checking all of your favorite websites by signing out of your accounts before you start homework. Make the browser you are working in full-screen size, so you can't see anything else on the monitor.

2. **Do not check your phone during meals and homework:** The cell phone can be the biggest downfall because you cannot always control when you get calls or text messages to distract you. Trust that any news can wait 30 minutes, turn your phone on silent, and put it on the other side of the room if you have to. Don't be "that guy" who is distracted and checking your phone while you are eating with other people.

> **TRUST THAT ANY NEWS CAN WAIT 30 MINUTES.**

Focus on genuine conversation and leave the phone in your pocket.

3. **Resist the urge to post everything online:** This generation is truly addicted to social media, and what comes with checking on your friends all the time is posting everything that comes into your head. Before you post on Facebook or Twitter try this: step away from the computer for 10 minutes and when you come back decide if that instance/event is still worth posting. "I'm eating a doughnut" might be tempting to post while you are in the moment, but will it be important to you or anyone else in 10 minutes? If our goal is to show Christ to the world, consider if your posts are bringing glory to God, or only aiming to bring glory to yourself.

MODESTY

Let's just be honest for a second (not that we haven't been throughout this book): walking around a college campus can be quite a surprise to some people. I'm not necessarily just talking about all the new things that college brings (like classes, schedules, and people); I'm referring to the way people dress.

You'll see a wide array of dress throughout the campus. You may even find yourself wishing there was a dress code at some points. It's bizarre to think about coming to a place where you actually wished there were people monitoring the grounds for bare midriffs and peak-a-boo boxers.

College is a strange place at times. The exact things you were excited to leave will be the same things you'll find yourself longing for. If you don't think this will be an issue, think again.

The way people dress is an outward expression of an inward reality. The way that someone views him/herself determines the effort they will put into their dress. Say goodbye to uniforms, and hello to expressive wardrobes.

As Catholics who know their dignity, it's important to remind ourselves that we should be dressing in a way that glorifies our God. The last thing we would want is to make others uncomfortable around us.

Ladies, it is not bad to want to look good – but it is better to turn a heart than it is to turn a head when we walk by. True beauty does just that. Men, it is not a bad thing to want to look strong or cool, but please be mindful that not everyone cares about the type of underwear you're wearing, nor do people want to see how big your shoulders are.

To dress more modestly may mean that you may be a little warmer than your

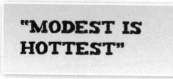

"MODEST IS HOTTEST"

fellow classmates with longer shirts and shorts, but, as they say, "Modest is hottest" (in more ways than one).

OUTREACH

Imagine walking into a class with an accidental black eye after a weekend long retreat. You got it after being elbowed (unintentionally) during some intense praise and worship. A classmate turns around as you sit down and whispers, "How did you get your black eye?"

You have a choice. You could either say, "Oh, you should see the other person," or be honest and say how you got it at a Catholic retreat praising the Lord. You're a little apprehensive to tell the story, but you do it anyways.

Unbeknownst to you, your classmate is a fallen-away Catholic who's had questions about God and the faith swirling in their head for months. Your black eye initiates a conversation about Catholicism, and eventually an accepted invitation to come to Mass with you. Seem too far out to believe? Trust me, it has happened.

More than likely, you will find yourself on a campus that has both Catholics and non-Catholics alike. This will be the case even if you're on a Catholic campus. There will be people who believe the same things as you and practice their faith, and there will be people who don't.

Similar to high school, you are called to be a witness of your faith in your dorm room, in your classes, on the sports field, and in every situation. God can use any situation to bring Him glory. He wants to use your life as a witness of His love. This is where things can get tricky, especially for those of you who are at a public university. It will be a constant struggle to try to live *in* the world without being *of* it.

HE WANTS TO USE YOUR LIFE AS A WITNESS OF HIS LOVE.

Here are some things to keep in mind when reaching out to your peers:

1. **Relational ministry:** Don't take for granted the relationships that you have with your peers. Even if you never say God's name, you are a witness of God's love for others simply by being you and authentically loving them. They will notice a difference and ask questions.

2. **The importance of the front porch:** If you're going to initiate an evangelistic conversation, start on the front porch. Find common interests and things they enjoy talking about that. At least in the South, people enjoy sipping on some sweet tea on the porch before walking into a house. In the same way, don't begin a conversation with something like, "Do you believe that Jesus is your Lord and Savior?" Try topics like sports, class, or weather and then ease into talking about faith.

3. **Three minute witness:** Practice your witness. People will ask you why you believe what you believe, so be ready to give a reason for your hope (1 Peter 3:4). If you can, try to keep it to three minutes. Practice it with friends and expect to say it at some point.

4. **The importance of the follow-up:** When reaching out to peers, you'll find that a lot of times people just want to be listened to. They may open up to you about some hurts in their life. It's important to follow up with them. Do what you can to remember their names. If necessary, write down notes after talking to them; the next time you see them, you'll remember to ask them about whatever you talked about in particular. It's also a good way to remember how to pray for them.

More than likely, your campus ministry program has ways that you can join their efforts to reach out to students. Evangelizing and reaching out is simply loving your neighbors and authentically caring about them.

PARENTS

You're in college – no more parents! Right? Wrong! Just because you're not sleeping under their roof doesn't mean they don't exist. College doesn't mean the end of your relationship with your parents; it means the beginning of a new chapter in your relationship.

You may have experienced some bumps along the way during your senior year in high school. Did you start to argue with your parents or want more freedom? You are not alone. That final year in high school can be tough – your parents may be struggling to let you have your independence and all you can think about is the day you gain your freedom. It causes a lot of tension.

Now that you are in college, especially in your freshman year, there will be some residual tension. On the one hand you want freedom, but now and again you know you've got to call Mom and Dad so you don't starve to death.

When it comes to your parents, try to communicate – call home at least once a week. While your parents are trying to respect your freedom, they'll have an easier time if you communicate with them. Use that cell phone you have and call home.

Something else to keep in mind: whether or not to go home during breaks. Before you go home, have a talk with your mom and dad about what is expected of you when you come home. While they may still not be ready to let you stay out all night without calling, they may be more comfortable letting you stay out later – if you promise to call.

This is a crazy thought: your parents do not exist to do your laundry and be an ATM machine. Yes, it is convenient to do laundry at home, but when you bring it home, don't drop and run. Spend some time with your parents and let them know how grateful you are for their help. Also, if you want your parents to treat you like an adult, show them you can handle money like an adult.

YOUR PARENTS WILL ALWAYS THINK OF YOU AS THEIR "BABY" REGARDLESS OF HOW OLD YOU ARE.

Here is something to keep in mind: your parents will always think of you as their "baby" regardless of how old you are. You are precious to them, even if you don't always get along.

Last but not least: take some time and say a prayer for your parents each day. Having an attitude of gratitude will go a long way in helping to develop a stronger relationship with your parents.

PEER PRESSURE

It's safe to say that in the years to come, just about every one of you will face peer pressure at some point. It doesn't always come in the way your parents warned you about though. Sometimes you may not even realize what's happening. But, if you succumb to this pressure you are giving away that very freedom that you had longed for so badly when you left high school.

IT DOESN'T ALWAYS COME IN THE WAY YOUR PARENTS WARNED YOU ABOUT.

When you hug your mom and dad good-bye and they are cramming in every last little piece of advice they can, take a mental note. Don't drink, don't do drugs, do your homework, and get to bed at a decent hour. Because as soon as the door closes your 'friends' have another plan for how you will spend your time at college.

Thank goodness God formed you with a conscience; you know when you should say yes and no. It's important that you listen to your gut feeling when you are asked to do or not do something. Take a second and think about your answer. Do I really want to do this? How will this affect me in the long run? Would God be happy with my decision?

Chances are you have already experienced some form of peer pressure. For some it maybe alcohol and sex and others it's staying out too late when you have a test the next day. You don't want to miss out during these next years having your face planted in textbooks, true. At the same time, you don't want to regret decisions you made in college or have to pay for them later on down the road. That's when it comes down to you making the decision and not your friends. As your parent's advice quietly plays over and over in the back of your mind, stop and think for a second. They really do have your best interest at heart.

The next morning when you wake up, sit down and ace that exam, that's when you realize, you are in control of your life. You made the decision that you felt was right and not your friends. Making wise decisions in the small things will help prepare you for the big decisions you'll have to eventually make, like your job, vocation, major, etc. Those seemingly small decisions prepare you for success. Those friends who stayed out too late, they sit there and struggle through that exam, while you, my friend, are preparing for life.

Make the most out of the years you are in college. What do you want to do and where do you want to go? You and God are the only ones who truly know what is best for you. Discover yourself and become who God intended you to be. Don't let others make that decision for you.

PRAYER

Pray without ceasing – a pretty tall order, right? And one made even more challenging as you struggle to adjust to new surroundings, new friends, roommates, classes, and all the other experiences that your first year in college will bring. But it's this very directive that can help smooth your transition and provide the peace that you need to have the best college experience possible, spiritually, and practically.

Remember, whether or not you have already chosen a major and have a pretty good idea about what you're going to do with your life, you are called to constantly discern God's will for you. Prayer is your relationship with God, and regular prayer will keep you growing closer to Him and better able to hear His voice in your life.

REGULAR PRAYER WILL KEEP YOU GROWING CLOSER TO HIM AND BETTER ABLE TO HEAR HIS VOICE IN YOUR LIFE.

Here are a few hints that will help you find time and make time to pray:

Establish a routine
Find the time that works best for you and put it in your schedule, just as you would a class or an appointment. If you're not a morning person, don't attempt a prayerful analysis of the latest papal document as soon as you open your eyes. Offer your thanks to God upon awakening and save more "demanding" prayer offerings for a time when you're more alert.

Find the prayer style that works for you
The many types of prayer the Catholic Church has for us to draw from are one of the most beautiful things about our faith. While attending Holy Mass at least weekly is the highest form of prayer that we can participate in, there are countless other ways to pray.

Here are a few:

- Rosary
- Liturgy of the Hours
- Chaplet of Divine Mercy
- Adoration
- Centering Prayer
- Lectio Divina
- Stations of the Cross
- Praise and Worship
- Prayers of Petition

If you're not familiar with any of these, you could look them up online or ask someone from your campus Newman Center or college parish. Find one or more that work for you.

Make your life a prayer

Understand that while its important to have uninterrupted prayer time in your life, there will be times (finals perhaps?) where you just can't seem to fit it in. That doesn't mean you can give up on prayer; just pray differently! Jot down the names of family and friends and offer them up to God for their needs and intentions. Say a decade of a rosary as you're walking to class. Offer your daily trials and struggles up to God for His intentions.

There are so many ways to incorporate prayer into your day no matter how busy you are. Find the time, routine, and type of prayer that works best for you and stick with it!

PROCRASTINATION

Procrastinating happens to the best of us. Sometimes, it happens only right before those final exams, or it's a habit done all the time. Most people struggle with procrastination, but how can you overcome it?

Study Space

Figure out where the best place for you to study is. However, if you immediately thought, "in my bed right before I go to sleep on Sunday," you might want to rethink your study methods. If you're studying in your bed, you're going to be falling asleep, trying not to fall asleep, or all of the above. So try to find a place where you can get the most work done. It might be the library, your desk, or even your friendly neighborhood coffee shop. But wherever it is, make sure it's a place with limited distraction.

FIGURE OUT WHERE THE BEST PLACE FOR YOU TO STUDY IS.

Studying Saturdays

Cramming all your weekend homework until the late hours of Sunday can be very tempting. But unless you want to be rushing through essay topics trying to figure out what you're even writing, try doing all your weekend homework on Saturday instead! You won't be rushed, and you'll have plenty of time to work on Sunday if you don't finish it all. More than likely, the only plan you'll have from that Saturday morning until noon is sleeping in. So find a good time either before or after lunch, and go attack that essay!

Study Buddies

Why do a good portion of students cheat in college? It's because they don't know the material. So avoid this heinous act of laziness and hang out with people who do understand what you're studying! Finishing a homework assignment with a group of friends, who are also being productive, can sometimes be the best way to free up time that you might have been spending procrastinating instead. Whether it's a couple of your friends, a tutor, or a study group, find the friends you click with well and go get your study on.

PROFANITY

What's the big deal with profanity? New words get created all the time, swears are just the same 26 letters arranged in a different order, right? Nope. How we talk gives others an impression of us. If we want to meet others who desire to live out their faith in college, we could turn someone off by our language before they even realize we're also striving to be holy. There may be professors who curse or say inappropriate things, but there may also be professors who think poorly of us if they overhear us swear.

People use swears as adjectives, nouns, verbs – you name it! We have to get more creative! College is a time we're supposed to become smarter, but swearing probably makes us look less intelligent. Instead of possibly offending someone by swearing when you drop that unnecessarily huge Biology book on your foot, use a non-offensive funny word and make someone laugh. Try "shucky darns!" or "oh snickerdoodle!" Make up a non-offensive word that will make your friends laugh.

Avoiding profanity is more than just making sure we don't swear. We can tear each other down or brighten someone's day by the way we talk. Words are so powerful. Ephesians 4:29 says, "No foul language should come out of your mouths, but only such as is good for needed edification, that it may impart grace to those who hear."

> **WE CAN TEAR EACH OTHER DOWN OR BRIGHTEN SOMEONE'S DAY BY THE WAY WE TALK.**

Think about a compliment someone gave you, or a time you were encouraged by someone's words. There's probably something positive someone has said to you along the way that has stuck with you.

And the same goes for negative language: someone gossiping about you or putting you down has probably bothered you. We can also be offensive in our language in the following ways:

- When we talk about good and holy topics like the human body or sex in a vulgar way

- When we use God's name in vain

- When we make light of hell

- When we use sarcasm or are condescending

There's enough negative talk surrounding us in college. Let's be different; be the example. Figure out what makes you use profanity or negative language, whether it's the music you listen to or the movies you watch. Replace them with better things. Don't make others doubt whether or not you're Christian; rather, be a witness! Let the words of your mouth be acceptable to the Lord (Psalm 19:14).

R.A.

It happens every year. You walk into your dorm for the first time and are greeted by someone sporting a school-colored polo and a nametag. They greet you and usher you up to your room for the first time. As they take time to welcome you to your dorm, they open the door to your room, give you a key, tell you that they are glad you are here, and then run through a law-book-sized list of rules and regulations.

After that lovely welcome, it is no wonder that R.A.'s, also known as Resident Advisor, get such an unusual reputation from their peers.

It is good to realize, whether you are just beginning your semester at school or are halfway through that your R.A. is there to help you. Many of the things they bring to your attention may seem unimportant to you, but there is a purpose and a meaning behind each of them. They enforce rules, like quiet hours, to maintain a good environment on the floor. If you are in need of anything they are usually a good person to go to with questions or concerns – especially if they have to do with the hall or a fellow resident.

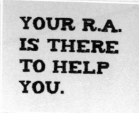

YOUR R.A. IS THERE TO HELP YOU.

Your R.A. should be your advocate amidst the school's residence staff. They speak up for what you need, and attempt to provide programs and activities that will help you to connect with your peers. Their role within a college environment, especially at a public institution, is crucial for you and they need your prayers.

Here are just a few tips for you when it comes to you and your dorm's Resident Assistant:

First, get to know them by name, not by crossing boundaries and getting in trouble, but by being proactive and learning who they are from the beginning. Touch base with them on a regular basis, to see if there is any important information you should know regarding upcoming events or information from the school itself. Be mindful of the rules that they must continually enforce; they may not seem to make sense, but there is a reason the school has deemed them worthy of enforcing.

Lastly, pray for them often, they need the Lord's guidance. Whether or not your R.A. is a faithful Christian, the Lord can still provide them with wisdom and insight for the tasks they are called to complete.

RELATIONSHIPS

Sometimes you find that special someone in high school and have to make the transition to college together, or you may find yourself in a relationship early in your college career.

Dating someone can be hard because of the new freedoms and independence there is in college. Learning how to put Christ in the center is the first step to truly making your relationship as fun and meaningful as it was meant to be.

Here are some tips:

1. **Pray together often.** Make Christ the rock of your relationship. Continually call each other to holiness and to deeper conversion. Start or end your dates with going to daily Mass together or taking a trip down to the Adoration chapel to do a holy half hour. Talk about what God is doing in your life and hold each other accountable.

2. **Know your boundaries and set rules.** There are no parents anymore to walk in every five minutes just to say "hey" when you guys are hanging out in your room. Leave the door in your apartment open when you both are inside, or go on a walk or run on campus instead of staying cooped up into your room. Make a rule that if one of you is on the bed, the other sits on a chair. There are plenty of creative ideas that vary from couple to couple, but the point is the same: do what it takes to stay pure.

3. **Communicate.** Openly talk with your boyfriend/girlfriend and be honest and intentional in knowing what is necessary to help your relationship stay holy and pure. Making purity a tabooed conversation only makes the elephant in the room larger than it has to be.

4. **Avoid temptation.** Don't set yourself up for failure. Don't watch a romantic movie on the couch when no one is home, when you can go out and see one in public. Avoiding situations that can

AVOIDING SITUATIONS THAT CAN LEAD TO TEMPTATION HELP BECAUSE YOU KICK THE POSSIBILITY OF FAILURE OUT OF THE PICTURE BEFORE THE DATE EVEN STARTS.

lead to temptation help because you kick the possibility of failure out of the picture before the date even starts.

5. **Utilize group dates.** They are an awesome way to have fun with your date while still having a great time with another couple, or some of your mutual friends.

6. **Learn to show healthy affection.** Be creative and surprising! Go on a picnic, write love letters, hold hands, cook dinner together, do the other person's favorite activity even if it's not your cup of tea, take a drive to a coast to watch a sunset, ask your priest if he would do a private Mass on your anniversary, go to Reconciliation together, do service trips together with your campus Newman Center or Catholic student group. Love is creative. There are so many ways to show affection outside of a make-out session (that mean a lot more), so keep your relationship fun by trying new things and surprising each other.

RESPONSIBILITY

When you were a kid, did you ever dream about what it would be like to be all grown up? Perhaps you pictured what kind of car you would drive or what job you would hold. Oh, the possibilities! But there is probably one concept that never entered into those fantasies: responsibility.

Time to Grow Up

Now that you're in college and on your own for the first time, it's time to grow up. All those things that your parents used to hold you accountable to are completely on your plate. It's up to you to attend Mass every Sunday and pray throughout the week. It's your job to remember to get to class on time and study. It's on you to ensure that you get a job and take care of your finances. Freedom is a beautiful thing, but it comes with a price called responsibility.

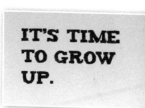

IT'S TIME TO GROW UP.

Consider the Consequences

Embracing responsibility is not an easy thing. There isn't necessarily anything fun about it. When you act responsibly, you typically don't get a medal, and no one will throw you a parade (although that would be awesome). But, when you act irresponsibly, everything changes. You messed up. You made a mistake, and people want answers.

Be sure to consider the consequences before you make decisions. How would you feel if you skipped Mass on Sunday? What could transpire if you didn't study for the big test? What would occur if you did rack up a large amount of debt? What could happen if you did get in a car with someone who had been drinking? By contemplating these possibilities, you will be sure to make wiser decisions.

Take Ownership

Above all, being responsible is about taking ownership of your life. By making good decisions you create good habits for yourself, which can only benefit you as you continue to grow and mature.

As St. Paul says in 1 Corinthians 13:11, "When I was a child, I used to talk as a child, think as a child, reason as a child; when I became a man, I put aside childish things." Now that you're in college it's time to grow up, put aside childish things, and be the person God has intended you to be.

SELF-IMAGE

Regardless of how old you are, there is a lot of time that goes into making sure that the way people perceive us is a reflection of who we are (or who we want to be). People will spend hours trying to come up with the perfect "about" section on Facebook, or pick a profile picture that accurately tells others what they want them to know about them (until, of course, there is a better picture).

Every person wants to be respected and accepted and, ultimately, loved. There is a God-shaped hole in each of our hearts that *infinitely* yearns for love. You'll find across the campus different examples of how people try to fill that hole with finite things, and the way that we view ourselves plays a huge role in the way we seek to fill that hole.

THERE IS A GOD-SHAPED HOLE IN EACH OF OUR HEARTS THAT *INFINITELY* YEARNS FOR LOVE.

Do we see ourselves as worthy of authentic love, or have we been hurt to the capacity that we believe that we deserve to suffer? If so, you'll probably find us sleeping around or putting up with things that others wouldn't because we don't see our worth.

Do we see ourselves as loveable, or do we think we have to earn people's respect and admiration? If so, you may find us trying really hard to be the funniest person in the room, or looking for perfection in our looks, grades, and talents.

Do we know the inherent dignity that we have, simply because we are God's? Our dignity does not rely on anything that we do: our grades, our dress, or our physique. Our dignity is a gift freely given to us by God at the moment of our conception. We did nothing to earn it.

> **TO KNOW WHO YOU ARE REQUIRES THAT YOU KNOW WHO GOD IS.**

To have a healthy self-image requires that you know who you are; to know who you are requires that you know who God is. It can be easy to love other people where they're at, but because God loves us we are called to love ourselves as well. That means to not put ourselves down and to uphold the dignity He gave us.

It can be easy to lose sight of how God views you because of the emphasis on worrying about how other people view you. But, if you could see yourself in the light that God sees you, you would know why He was willing to die for you.

There is no one else who could be you better than you can. Only His infinite love can satisfy your infinite desires. Let Him be the mirror in which you view yourself.

Be confident in who God made you to be and let *that* determine your self image.

SEXUALITY

Do you realize that your body is actually speaking a language? It speaks of awe-inspiring realities; the true meaning behind you being male or female. Contentment in a relationship – in fact, in all of life – comes down to whether you are telling a truth with the language of your body or telling a fib.

What lingo does your body actually speak? What is the theology that your body is pointed toward? Male and female bodies, just in the fact that they are gendered, speak a language of gift. Contrary to what may be going on in the dorm room next door to you, this gift is to be shared exclusively within the Sacrament of Marriage between a man and a woman.

> **YOU DISCOVER YOUR TRUE SELF ONLY BY MAKING YOURSELF A SINCERE AND TOTAL GIFT TO ANOTHER.**

As a human you discover your true self only by making yourself a sincere and total gift to another. This is imprinted in your very body as male or female: a man's body, for example, does not make sense except in relation to a woman's body and vice versa. The very parts of a man's body that mark his masculinity are designed so that he can give himself away (make a gift of himself) to a woman. A woman's body is designed so that she in turn can make a gift of herself to a man. This is the only thing that makes total sense of the very parts of her body that mark her femininity.

Male and female bodies are intended to fit together. But along with the body comes the mind, heart, emotions: your total self.

An issue you will most likely have dealt with, or will deal with in some way, is encountering people who think sexuality is relative. The homosexual lifestyle has attained a kind of romanticism in society today. It enjoys charter status in the popular sections of cosmopolitan areas, inside the art house division of the entertainment industry, and on many university campuses.

As Catholics, we are called to be compassionate and to love the sinner, not the sin. We cannot forget that God created the sexes to complement each other – not only physically, but also emotionally and spiritually. A heterosexual couple is called to chastity prior to marriage. In the same way, if someone has same sex attraction, they are held to the same moral standards as every one else prior to marriage.

Marriage is a divine institution created by God between a male and a female. It reflects the totality of God's love, which is freely given to us; without reservation He faithfully gives Himself to His bride, the Church. The fruit from His love is that we can share of it.

Marriage between a man and a woman reflects that same free, total, faithful, and fruitful love that God has with His bride.

SINGLE & READY TO MINGLE

Entering college single could be considered either a great thing or a curse, depending on your outlook. Being single is an incredible gift that many people seem to misunderstand. However, when the time comes for you to date (if you are called to marriage), here are some tips:

> **BEING SINGLE IS AN INCREDIBLE GIFT.**

- **Grow in your faith and in knowing who you are:** Finding your identity is the underlying purpose of college. You only have one time in your life to truly go on this exploration with God in getting to know what type of person you are called to be. Don't waste it by wishing you had someone to hold hands with; embrace it!

- **Trust God to protect your heart:** When you're not committed to someone, it can be easy to fixate your eyes on more than a couple people. Intentionally pray for emotional purity so that God will guard your heart and save it for the right person.

- **Include God in the entire decision making process.** Pray individually before dates (and why not ask him/her to go to the chapel with you?).

- **Be upfront about who you are in the beginning.** There is no sense in trying to hide who you are and that you have a relationship with Christ. Letting the other person know about your faith and your views on purity will be beneficial – it will either turn into a red flag or a better understanding of what you both have in common!

- **Set your bar high** (and reasonable) for the type of person you desire to date. Don't settle for those who don't make the cut. When you know what you deserve, it can help you find those who actually have the right intentions for dating you.

- **Remember who you are called to be in a relationship** and rise up to meet it. Your bar should be just as high as your significant other's.

- **Don't let dating someone become your only reality.** Keep friends and family close. Don't lose sight of other people in your life because of your new (and exciting) addition. The last thing you want is to only have the support of the person whom you are dating.

- **Don't think anyone single and in a pew is whom God is calling you to.** If someone has a strong faith it does not mean that they will always be right for you. There are plenty of people who are religious like you are, so don't settle for the first one who looks your way.

- **Be patient.** Don't let yourself grow anxious looking for someone. God's timing is always better than ours.

- **Be yourself!** This is one of the most important things. If you're clumsy or quirky, God knows someone in this world will find it adorable every time you make a corny joke, or trip over your own feet. You are beautifully and wonderfully made, and someone will love every beauty and wonder that you come with.

SLEEP

Sleep can be your best friend or your worst enemy; but, ultimately, it's up to you to decide how it will affect your life. Whether you're a studying machine or a party animal, you need sleep.

Before you take these words too far and go take a mini-coma next weekend, consider using these recommendations to build better sleeping habits:

Be Consistent

The more consistent your sleep habits are, the more your body will thank you for it. So, if you're staying up until 3:00 AM every day and on weekends you crash until two in the afternoon, you can be sure your body will be exhausted the next time you have to wake up for that eight o'clock class. If you need to wake up early, don't be hanging out in your friend's dorm room for two or three hours because you're bored; go to bed! And if you're a night owl, then take later classes so you can sleep in. College classes take place at many different times during the day, from noon to night, so take advantage of being able to choose your class schedule.

Naps

Sometimes as a student you don't have enough time to get a full night's rest. That's when naps are most useful! A nap during the day can be exactly what you need to recharge and finish the day out strong. The trick is figuring out the right time in your day to take a nap. Taking a nap during your Biology class, or any class for that matter, may not be such a wise decision. Also don't take a snooze too late, because you might just pass out until the next day and miss that date with the only person you have chemistry with in Chemistry, or you may miss the next big assignment that was due.

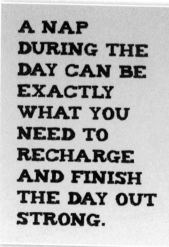

A NAP DURING THE DAY CAN BE EXACTLY WHAT YOU NEED TO RECHARGE AND FINISH THE DAY OUT STRONG.

Go to Bed

College is very exciting, but don't forget that the most important part of getting good sleep is to go to bed. Sometimes you might have to pull the dreaded all-nighter to study for that exam that you only have one page of notes for. But your body needs at least 7 hours of sleep, so although you might not always hit that magical number, do your best to at least get as close to that number as possible.

Keep track of your sleeping patterns, and keep them consistent; if you do, your body will thank you for it later.

SOCIAL MEDIA

Have a Facebook, Twitter, or Youtube account? According to recent surveys, over 90 percent of college freshmen enter college with at least one social media account. Most college students find out more about what major events are going on in the world via social media connections than any other way. Your college professors may even use social media to teach and inform.

The main thing you need to remember is this: what goes online stays online. It's that simple. A digital record will exist that will most likely follow you through your entire life. So what might seem like a funny thing to post while at a gathering one Friday night of your sophomore year might not be what you want your potential future spouse, bosses, constituents, neighbors, or children viewing one day. Your college most likely did a digital social media search when you applied; future employers are likely to do the same.

WHAT GOES ONLINE STAYS ONLINE.

The Second Vatican Council called communication media "marvels" and "gifts" from God, but it also recognized that these gifts can be mixed blessings, depending on how they are used.

With all that in mind, here are a couple ideas of how you can best use social media:

1. **Apply Gospel Values.** Ask yourself whether the media you are using foster a sense of the divine, of your obligation to forgive and your need for forgiveness. Is compassion, reconciliation, thanksgiving, and moral responsibility affirmed with what you are posting, liking, sharing, and tweeting?

2. **Use Your Intelligence.** As entertaining and useful as social media can be, it should not be accepted uncritically or thoughtlessly. In subtle and not so subtle ways, social media can convey moral messages. Think about what is portrayed and why. How does

it relate to Christian faith and moral belief? If something seems shocking, is anything of value also being conveyed? Is comedy used for genuine amusement or merely as a put-down? Are your social media choices leading you or others closer to Christ?

3. **Talk to People.** People are more important than things. Social media usage can help build community where people can get out of themselves and toward each other. Ask yourself whether your way of using media does or isolates you instead. Look for ways to balance screen time with time spent face to face with others.

TEACHERS

"That's how we know that the Gospels are false and Jesus was not God."

Day three into your New Testament course, and the professor just trashed the entire Christian faith in one sentence.

You may have professors who don't teach the way you like or seem lazy, but hopefully you never have one that attacks your faith. Unfortunately, there are many professors who think the best way to express "intelligence" is to slam religion. So when the heresy starts getting spewed, what do you do?

As a Catholic you are called to stand up for the Truth – the challenge is your professor has a fancy degree and believes that entitles him/her to spit out garbage and call it "knowledge." If you get frustrated and try to argue, you will probably get shut down because you "don't know anything." Don't get mad – get reading. Take notes on things you disagree with or have questions about and research them. Ask a local priest or campus minister to help you. This takes time in addition to studying, but it will help you stay rooted in the Truth. With this knowledge you can contest points of heresy in a scholarly fashion rather than with blind anger. If you are continually shut down, rejoice; Jesus and the apostles also were shut down by a lot of "smart" people.

DON'T GET MAD - GET READING.

But, if you take your situation and use it as a time for growth, your professor may actually come to respect your opinion, though they may still disagree. By the end of my class that is what happened, and I was able to give a voice to other Christian students who couldn't stand up for their faith.

So if that day comes when your professor begins to toss out some heretical nonsense, take a deep breath and grab your *Catechism*. You've been given a chance to grow in your faith and defend the Truth.

TEST STRESS

Here is a little well-known fact: panic moments (such as waiting until the last second to study or write a paper) cause an increase of adrenaline in the body. What is adrenaline about? Fight or flight! Your higher-level brain functions shut down. Plan ahead and study! You need to be a good steward of the money you are spending at college (or the money you've received from a scholarship or grant).

You already know this, but the best test-taking advice is to take plenty of time to be prepared. Waiting until the last minute and cramming notes as you walk to class will only leave you more panicked and doubtful.

Forming a study group can also help with preparing for a test. As a group, you can help each other with notes, quiz each other, and discuss important issues from class. Plus, you'll have a built in accountability group that can help keep you on task.

Talk with your professor and get to know him/her. Professors keep office hours for students to stop by, so make good use of their time.

If you have not yet developed good study habits, it's not too late. For many of us, studying usually takes place with lots of music, television on, Facebook lurking, and our cell phones lighting up with text messages. How much are you really able to take in when you study like that? Find a study environment that allows you to really focus.

IF YOU HAVE NOT YET DEVELOPED GOOD STUDY HABITS, IT'S NOT TOO LATE.

Nothing is worse than showing up for a test and falling asleep halfway through. Make sure you sleep the night before your test. Once again, the brain starts to shut down when you're exhausted. No amount of caffeine is going to really fix that. You can slam back a couple of 24-hour energy drinks and it'll keep you up, but it won't necessarily keep you sharp.

Here is something important you should know: colleges have ways to help you with your test taking. If you already know that you have test taking anxiety, let someone help you with that. Many college campuses have centers where you can get some help. These centers offer a more calming environment for taking your test and sometimes give you more time to take certain tests. Check 'em out!

Spend some time in front of the Blessed Sacrament. Be still and know that He is God and you are not. Remember the Gifts of the Holy Spirit: wisdom, knowledge, and understanding. Now would be a good time to ask the Lord to stir up those gifts within you.

TIME MANAGEMENT

You are staring at a blank Microsoft Word document at 2:17 AM in your school's library on a Thursday night. The reason? You have an eight-page research paper that you haven't started due at 8:00 AM tomorrow.

Your mind turns to all the things you did instead of this paper over the past two weeks: you remember staying up late with your friends playing video games, time spent on weekends hanging out with your boyfriend or girlfriend, and that Saturday afternoon *Lord of the Rings* marathon. You realize that those things were probably not the best ways to use your time, but there is nothing you can do about it now. That 8:00 AM deadline isn't moving, and your paper won't write itself. It's going to be a long night.

The amount of freedom you have in college is wonderful; you don't have your parents telling you not to hang out with friends until homework is finished, professors aren't constantly reminding you about due dates, and you can wear sweatpants to class. Freedom to set your own schedule is great, but can quickly translate into long nights and poor grades if you don't learn how to manage your time effectively.

If you want to avoid the late night, poorly done paper and learn how to manage your time early on, here's how:

Get a Planner and Make Study Time

Buy a good academic planner before the semester begins. Ideally, this will have a section for every day of the week and a full calendar at the beginning of each month. When you receive an assignment for class, write down the due date in your planner immediately. Set aside study time in your planner that allows enough time for your class reading, weekly assignments, and any long-term projects.

> **IF YOU SET SEVERAL SMALL "MILESTONES" FOR BIG ASSIGNMENTS IN ADVANCE OF DUE DATES, YOU ARE MORE LIKELY TO GET A GOOD GRADE.**

Set Milestones

If you set several small "milestones" for big assignments in advance of due dates, you are more likely to get a good grade. If you have a final paper due at the end of the semester, set personal "internal" dates in your planner for when you will have your research completed, finish a rough draft, and even a time to talk with the professor to see if you are on the right track.

Learn to Say No

This is the greatest discipline you can learn. You can set all your milestones and set aside study time, but if you drop it all the moment your roommate wants to go see a movie, that paper won't get done. You may feel like you are missing out, but by saying "no," you are exercising true freedom and saying "yes" to getting a good grade.

Imagine this: It's a Thursday night and you are relaxing with a group of friends. Your final paper is completed and done well. You see a couple of your friends walk by your room and ask them to join you, but they respond, "Can't, we are going to be in the library all night working on our final papers."

Where would you rather be?

CONCLUSION

College life is not going to be easy, no matter how hard you pray, how often you go to Mass, or how fervently you try to love God. He doesn't promise us an easy life and that's okay. Struggles keep us reliant on God. Struggles increase our discipline. Struggles build character. You don't have to worry about a life filled with struggle if God is with you. You need only worry about a life without God.

Many times life is difficult because we are trying to fit into the world, and just don't feel like we do. That's because you were not created for this world, you were created for the next one. Jesus reminds us to be in the world but not of the world (John 15:18-19).

To be holy means to be "set apart." As you allow God to make you more and more holy throughout college, you are allowing God to set your life apart even more. That doesn't mean you have to go live a secluded life by yourself though, it means that your life stands out, as a light to all those in the world trapped in darkness. The goal is not to fit in; it's to stand out (humbly) in holiness and in love.

This call to holiness shouldn't stress you; it should excite you. A good portion of our lives are spent stressing about things that already happened (which we can't change) or about things that might happen (which we can't control). God doesn't want you to be filled with anxiety and stress (Matthew 6:34). Share your days with Him. Share your stresses with Him. Spend time talking (and more importantly) listening to Him. Seek out true friendships (Sirach 6:14) and community with others who believe in God like you do, and who are seeking God as you are (2 Corinthians 6:14).

College is a time for growth and as your move forward in life, your faith should move with you. This will require discipline and you are capable of being a witness on your college campus.

Life Teen wants to help support you and to foster that community of support. Go on our website and find a parish in your area. Check out the national events that we host, spend some time at our summer camps as a summer missionary, and look for regional prayer meetings and training opportunities coming to your area. Become a member of our online community.

Life Teen is here to walk with you as we all journey toward Christ!

SPECIAL THANKS

A special thanks to those who have contributed to the Forward Thinking section:

Anna Albert	*Kevin Hickey*
Natalie Alemán	*Christina Mead*
Nicole Alemán	*Chris Mueller*
Mark Bocinski	*Derek Natzke*
Amy Brant	*Eric Porteous*
Catie Disser	*Randy Raus*
Paige Dowler	*Joan Root*
Kevin Fenter	*Erika Rosa*
Melissa Ginther	*Rachel Shank*
Jess Givens	*Michael Specht*
Jon Givens	*Joel Stepanek*
Mark Hart	*Gabriel Telepak*
Katie Heller	*Chris Turner*